W9-BQI-100

The Journal of Black Masculinity

Editor & Founder: C. P. Gause, University of North
                            Carolina, Greensboro

Book Editor: Robert E. Randolph, University of
                            North Carolina, Greensboro

Copy & Layout Editor: Jean K. Rosales, University of North
                            Carolina, Greensboro

Associate Editor in Residence: Ruth Reese, University of North
                            Carolina, Greensboro

Associate Editor in Residence: Pamela Fitzpatrick, University of North
                            Carolina, Greensboro

The Journal of Black Masculinity

C. P. Gause, Founder and Editor

The Journal of Black Masculinity is a peer-reviewed international publication providing multiple discoursed and multiple-discipline-based analyses of issues and/or perspectives with regard to black masculinities. The journal invites the following submissions for consideration: empirical, theoretical, and literary scholarship as well as essays, poetry, and art. Manuscripts from multiple disciplines beyond the humanities and social sciences are encouraged. *The Journal of Black Masculinity* is published three times a year and has a ten percent (10%) acceptance rate. *The Journal of Black Masculinity* also publishes special issues on a periodic basis with guest editors focusing on themed issues.

Manuscript submissions, books for review, and correspondence concerning all editorial matters should be sent to: C. P. Gause, Editor, *Journal of Black Masculinity,* using the contact information below. Manuscripts submitted for publication will be peer-reviewed.

Manuscripts should be submitted in electronic form and should not exceed 35 pages in length (including endnotes and references). Authors should follow the *APA Publication Manual*, 6th edition (APA Press, 2010). A style guide for preparing manuscripts is located on the *JBM* website at http://www.blackmasculinity.com.

Journal of Black Masculinity ©GES Publishing Group
GES LLC
2309 W. Cone Blvd. Suite 142
Greensboro, NC 27408
www.blackmasculinity.com
drcpgause@gmail.com
336.509.6171

The Journal of Black Masculinity

Copyright © 2011 GES Publishing Group/GES LLC.

ISBN 978-1-60910-584-6

ISSN 2158-9623

Printed in the United States of America.

Volume 1, No. 2

Spring 2011

Toby Jenkins
George Mason University

Michael Jennings
University of Texas at San Antonio

Ralph Soney
Roanoke-Chowan Community College

Lemuel Watson
Northern Illinois University

The Journal of Black Masculinity

Volume 1, No. 2   Spring 2011

Contents

Contextualizing the (Re) Presentations of Black Masculinity

C. P. Gause, Ph.D.
Editor, *The Journal of Black Masculinity*

Engaging in teaching, leading, and learning that is transformative and activist oriented will often create moments of anxiety and fear. Fear is a crippling state of being. It operates from the perspective of no surprises and the desire to be aware of every move, position, and thought. I developed an acrostic for the word FEAR: Forever Entrapped And Robbed. Although the United States is more ideologically, philosophically, culturally, linguistically, racially, and ethnically diverse than any given point in her history, many of her citizens are currently living in a state of fear. The terrorist attacks of September 11, 2001, our government's response to Hurricane Katrina on August 29, 2005, the global economic crisis of 2008-2009, and the election of our nation's first African American president, Barack H. Obama, the Gulf Oil Spill, and the horrible acts of violence that include the mass shooting in Tucson, Arizona on January 8, 2011 will shake the very core of most of us. Is there any hope in the United States for solidarity and change? While nations in the Middle East are holding peaceful demonstrations calling for changes in their government, we continue to struggle with distortions, political un-rest, partisan politics, and the (re) segregation of public schools. Much of this is witnessed at lightening speed via the Internet, social networking sites, and "the cloud."

Over the past forty years, scholars have engaged the question of how best to educate the nation's citizenry regarding diversity, equity, and inclusion. Many have researched practices for teachers and educators to better engage in multicultural education and culturally responsive teaching. Moreover, the past five decades of education has become the un-kept promise of our society. Children of color and in poverty continue to be the victims of failing schools, inadequately prepared teachers, and the recipients of inequitable learning conditions. Given the present structure of the nation's public schools, the majority of ethnic/linguistic minorities will never realize their dreams—life, liberty, and the pursuit of happiness. Don't get me wrong—gains have been made and many minorities have benefitted from programs and initiatives instituted by local, state, and federal legislation. However, as the population of the United States increases ethnically and racially, separation by class and race is more evident in our public schools, which will continue to leave children of color and children in poverty behind.

This issue brings together scholars, practitioners, and community activists who provide various insights and perspectives regarding black masculinity within broad constructs. Issues regarding race, representation, and regionalism are presented, as well as frameworks regarding policy, popular culture, and pedagogy. I hope you find their work to be engaging and enlightening.

Dear Racism

Brett Lesley Cumberbatch
Ontario Institute for Studies in Education at the University of
Toronto
Toronto, Canada

Dear Racism,

You and I have been chilling for a while
Over the years, you adapt, you change styles
I heard you play a beautiful mind
George Jackson knew that
Other times you play crab
Climb up, around, and over my peoples back
Now you got us on wrap, just listen to rap

Behind the bars of my mind my hopes flow dark
Reaching for light while standardized scores turn me Right
"*You got potential son*", so mimic the words proposed as bright
I sit in spaces with so called class mates seeing me as critical material
Their mouths speak but how many of them would blend with me?
Participating yeah, but never integrate or authentically befriend me
Only in group settings with data collection on the table- what a fable

My spirit has scabbed over and my blood turn cold hearing them
conduct doctorate talks
About people who look like me, talk like me, and cry like me
The resulting resolutions
I will never learn, be equal, or earn Respect
Research ourselves, aid ourselves, and teach ourselves, out of the
question

How else can someone right a racist participatory action piece on how
to spy on us?
Was it fate or greed that led them to believe, with, for, in, or against us?

That all we can do is breed, bleed, and never at their metric levels read
Someday soon or not
I will sit in front of a jury
Granting me ethics to look at my fellow people
Who will judge them on their unethical treatment?
Who indeed, I say with a post racial Negro toned please
Not someone who likes me!

I've sat in the seat of supposed knowledge
Twisting, listening to inorganic thoughts produce organic lies
And plant the seeds that will build the future body lies
Of the young men who are put in Black bags
I guess these words act like twisty ties
I've sat in a chair, with a Chair, lost and spoken to as
If I am nothing while name plates supposedly state something

It was systemic déjà-vu
Because I watched a man and woman do it to a young boy of colour in
kindergarten too
I guess we both belong to the going nowhere in education crew
The only people moving up are those who talk about being equal to us-
you know, me plus you
They bring in the books with our kids on the cover
"Let's deficit education together"
Talk in sweet voices compassionate like 1890's missionary
anthropology lovers

But when I straw poled them over tea 2 see if they would pair me with
their seed
The complexion of the sea surrounding the pupil of their eyes
exclaimed it all

There's a special place in my heart for black men who hate other Black men
"I didn't come into this world a slave so I will strive to be a man
Everyone in my vicinity should know where and how we/I stand
It's going to happen anyways, I'll never fit in, and so I accept I have to stand out
Where I come from everyone who dies to fit in, lives their lives begging for handouts"

Biography

Brett Lesley Cumberbatch is the president and a founding partner of STGC Consulting Ltd. He is an internationally regarded urban education consultant. He holds a Hon. B.A. in History from the University of Toronto (Trinity College) and a M.Ed. from the Ontario Institute for Studies in Education at the University of Toronto, where he is currently a Ph.D. candidate.

www.smashtheglassceiling.com
brett@smashtheglassceiling.com

The Stuff Of Sway And Nightmares

~for Joseph Danitca[1]

"There's no such thing as arrested or frustrated hope." —EJ
Raines

my love sits hence withering on the vine,
and is a quick loss of livelihood,
a mother tongue stayed by a stray calling;
i am bound for america from haiti.
i conceal my fear as child and as father,
meeting opposite families of life and ambition
on opposite shores of grief and instinct

i am bound for america from haiti.
exile means meant to die here,
a painful sentiment spoken aloud
among buried countries and illusions

my tombstone imagines gestures of my mind
and shouts a hesitated hope;
for i am bound for america from haiti
without assurance of destination or duration

And I say to you:
brother, am I not traumatized enough?

> brother, do I not extend my hand?
> brother, am I not dying?

1. In 2004, Joseph Dantica fled Port-au-Prince, Haiti and sought political asylum in Miami, Florida. Incidentally, he and his son were detained at a U. S. Homeland Security detention center. Dantica became ill and was refused medical care because the medics thought he was faking his illness; tragically, Dantica died five days after his arrival in the United States. His benevolent life and tragic death are chronicled in Edwidge Danticat's memoir *Brother, I'm Dying* (2007).

Biography

Robert E. Randolph, Jr. lectures at the University of North Carolina at Greensboro in the African American Studies Program. He is also an aspiring novelist and poet. He is currently laboring on a novel, *The Crooke Mile*, which delves into the often neglected subject of black male childhood sexual abuse. He can be contacted at rrandolph7@gmail.com.

Two Poems

Tony Lamair Burks II
San Diego, CA

InHeaven&Hale

InHale.

Your smell, your touch.

ExHale.

Your scent, your embrace.

InHale.

Your smile, your laugh
All cause me to inHale, to breathe
And it feels like I'm in paradise, like I'm inHeaven
With
You.

one...embrace

together
in time
in space
despite distance
without embrace

us
me
you
we

seek ways
to transform two
in
to
one...embrace

Biography

When not serving students and adults as an area superintendent with the nation's eighth largest public school district, Dr. Tony Lamair Burks II can be found eating and cooking the world over. An avid reader, CrossFitter, storyweaver, and master whistler, he has written three books for children and young adults, and he wants to become a chef and own a "bed and brunch" when he retires from education.

The Critical Nature Of Black Men In The Academy

Dr. Michael E. Dantley
Miami University

This paper was presented at the 21ˢᵗ Annual Conference on African American Culture and Experience co-organized by Dr. C. P. Gause and convened at the University of North Carolina at Greensboro, October 14-16, 2010. The theme of the conference was "Exploring Black Masculinity Across Multiple Landscapes: A Global Perspective."

I am very pleased to have been invited to keynote at this signature event, the 21ˢᵗ annual conference on African American Culture and Experience. What a powerful occasion this is to have this number of Black brothers, Black intellectual brothers in one place, at one time, talking and thinking, sharing and reflecting on our journeys in the academy. Such an amalgamation of Black thinkers and intellectuals ought to hopefully spell some kind of alarm to those who would otherwise minimize as well as exoticize our gathering together. What our coalescing, during this brief period of time, must do is to establish a formidable and yet radical agenda to achieve a number of things.

First, the agenda must include how the work of teaching, scholarship, and service can serve as a political, a revolutionary political vehicle to upset hegemonic notions of race, class, gender, ability, sexual orientation that are solidly ensconced in the very fabric of the academy. The rhetoric of diversity is oftentimes merely that, rhetoric. Too often, diversity, in all of its facets, becomes a perpetual goal, some ethereal construct never intended to be realized or operationalized. But it appeases the neo-liberal consciousness that undergirds much of the work in the academy. It affirms some misguided notion that if we as a university are at least thinking about diversity and make a vehement declaration that we are committed to diversity, we are at least doing something and not placating the racist, classist, homophobic, xenophobic foundations that generally underpin the lyrics of the university's voice. So our work during and following this conference has to take on a revolutionary tenor. It must be about upsetting the status quo and deeply infusing a voice of resistance and reconstruction through the work celebrated in higher education.

Second, our work together during this momentous kairos moment must be to release organic intellectuals to engender a civil rights agenda that not only impacts the university but society writ large. It is vitally important that we position our work in a critical space that asks the question of whose interests are being served through these academic machinations and how can our work not only expose the structures and processes that create and promote asymmetrical relations of power but also bring them down. I believe the work of Cornel West will be exceptionally helpful as he assists us to embrace the dilemma of the Black intellectual and establishes four distinct ways to think about Black men and intellectual work.

Third, I believe that all of this work must be motivated by a principled, purposive, and pragmatic paradigm that is grounded in a radical, more socially just notions of spirituality, critical spirituality, specifically.

May I delve into these issues by first delineating the conceptual framework as well as the experiential context that frames today's remarks. I have been a Black man for decades and, no matter what position I have held, many of the socio-political dynamics have remained consistent. My qualifications for position have always been second-guessed; my self-perpetuation of the Black man has to work twice as hard and produce twice as much—a family heritage, I might add, keeps the work doable but, at times, the socio-political dynamics almost become overwhelming. My goal is not to bore you with this autobiography but to simply briefly contextualize and historicize myself in such a way that my comments are linked to some relevant ambient and you more clearly see where I am coming from.

Allow me to cite one example from my days as an elementary school principal. I was the principal of a neighborhood school in inner city Cincinnati. The school building was old, in disrepair, and predominantly Black. In Cincinnati, when I was a principal, those descriptors were pretty much pervasive—old, irreparable building; Black students. My building was cursed with metal steps so that, every time it rained or snowed, my students would fall down the steps in quantum numbers. I grew tired of sending hurt students home from involuntarily cascading down dangerously wet steps, so I called the buildings and facilities assistant superintendent and simply requested that treading be applied to my metal steps. I failed to pass this request through my immediate supervisor, an African American woman, who became livid because of my oversight. She came at me as though I had committed one of the seven unpardonable sins and, indeed, in her mind, I had. I had dissed her. Now, I know there were some gender dynamics at work then but I was not, at that time, wise enough nor sophisticated enough to have named them. But I had gotten the tread on the steps and my students had stopped falling. So for me, despite my procedural transgression, everyone won.

After that year, I was moved not more than a mile and a half, same neighborhood, to become the principal of a magnet school. This magnet school had been created to implement the court desegregation order our school district was under. The practical goal was to convince white parents to place their children in this predominantly Black school in this Black neighborhood. So, without hesitation, the superintendent came to my school and informed that I only needed to make requests to him for whatever I needed for my school. I was able to hand-select my faculty, buy new equipment; whatever I needed was at my disposal, including a brand new building. This was so different from my experience as the principal of a neighborhood school. Everything changed when my role was to recruit white children to my school.

For some time after that, I was plagued with the dynamics of those two divergent situations. The juxtaposition between the two, in my mind, needed some rational resolution. And the only explanation, to me, was institutional and blatant racism. While racism in and of itself is damning enough, I felt that, concomitantly, there were other confounding complexities at play in these two situations.

When I became an assistant professor at Miami University, my first office there was sandwiched between Drs. Peter McClaren and Henry Grioux. Through the crevices of my office walls flowed the tenets of critical theory. And it was through critical theory that I was able to, as Paulo Freire argued, read the word and the world, to actually name the injustices that I had lived through. So I embraced critical theory as the most advantageous way for me to think about what was happening in reality in schools. Critical theory helped me to name the asymmetrical relations of power and the debilitating and disenfranchising machinations of hegemony, as well as the determined agenda of the social and political status quo that grounded the work of schools to marginalize, discriminate, and perpetuate a capitalist agenda. So I come to this keynote assignment fully aware that at work in the academy are racism, sexism, classism, homophobia, xenophobia, and other forms of labeling while concomitantly minimizing the other. So I will build the rest of my remarks from a critical frame, but also a critical spiritual and prophetically pragmatic grounding as espoused by the eminent Black scholar, Cornel West.

I would like to look at what Cornel West calls the dilemma of the Black intellectual. I believe that much of what West has articulated some time ago, when his essay on the Black intellectual was written, is relevant even in these contemporary times. At first, I was not going to delineate three of the four models West outlines as the categories of Black intellectuals. But as I thought more of it, I realized that a quick covering of three of the four might help each of us to situate ourselves, even if very loosely, to how we see ourselves and how we wage the on-going fight as Black, intellectual men in the academy. West actually outlines four models of the Black intellectual, those being the bourgeois model: the Black intellectual as humanist, the Marxist model: the Black intellectual as revolutionary, the Foucaultian model: the Black intellectual as postmodern skeptic and, finally, the Insurgency model: the Black intellectual as critical, organic catalyst.

The bourgeois model of the Black intellectual follows the frames and contexts of the hegemonic notions of the academy. It prizes the legitimation process through degrees, certificates, and position. It sees placement in the white-dominated academy as something to be celebrated, something to be tenaciously sought after because it spells for some the status of having arrived, of having been accepted in academe, of having made it. No doubt, there is some intellectual benefit to be gained through this process of legitimation, though the legitimation costs. Too often, in order for the Black intellectual to be tenured and promoted, the official badge of legitimation in the academy, one has to make choices and decisions that can often be filled with a plethora of "what if" anxieties. What if my research is Afro-centric; will that hurt me? What if my pedagogical style is not only intellectually rigorous but also indeed exceptionally challenging? Am I over-compensating for the inbred racist stereotypes that are alive and well in the academy especially as they relate to the brothers? I like how West says, "There is always the need to assert and defend the humanity of Black people, including their ability and capacity to reason logically, think coherently and write lucidly." Even if the bourgeois intellectual has been afforded entrance through the legitimation process, he must also recognize, as West puts it, "This hostile environment results in the suppression of their critical analyses and in the limited use of their skills in a manner considered legitimate and practical."

If the Black male intellectual embraces the bourgeois model, he has, in my opinion, been co-opted and commodified with little more to show for his labor than promotion and tenure or the celebration of academe. I recognize that I sit perched in a privileged position, being a full tenured professor, but I also sit here with the plethora of experiences, the sometimes excruciating self-reflection and personal inquisition of my own motivations and wonderings about the professional decisions I made in order to sit here. I had to determine how writing about the plight of Black children in urban schools under the auspices of neo-liberal and conservative regimes of leadership thought would impact my potential to be promoted and tenured. I had to deeply consider how unashamedly writing about spirituality—that is, a spirituality grounded in an African American prophetic tradition—would play to editors who might find my work not scholarly enough, pedantic, and trivial. But two things remained constant for me. First, I had to be true to my genuine or sacred self. I could not hide in the covers of acceptability and the reification of the status quo but believed that my work had to open new frontiers and cross borders in order to cause educational leadership to have a more critical and impacting voice. Second, I had to write from my experience. I had to write from the depths of my soul about the issues that mattered most to me and that I deemed responsive to the needs of people who look like me. That was the risk, but it was an essential risk I had to take in order to produce my best work possible.

The second model of the Black intellectual Cornel West defines is the Marxist model or the revolutionary intellectual. I must share with you that I have never considered myself to be a Marxist, though the tenets of critical theory that have Marxist leanings have helped me to frame my intellectual inquiries and to name the world I've come to know. But indeed, there are shortcomings to grounding a Black intellectual perspective in a Marxist frame. Our issues cannot be confined to a social/structural polemic as Marxism celebrates. Marxism—while liberating the intellectual to develop a critical consciousness that deconstructs, troubles, and demystifies bourgeois underpinnings of societal functions and helps us to concretize our radical and revolutionary perspectives— remains, as West argues, "divorced from the integral dynamics, concrete reality and progressive possibilities of the Black community." Indeed, it is revolutionary thought without a pragmatic agenda. Black intellectuals must think critically, must ask the poignant questions, and must tie those inquiries with the vagaries of life for a Black human being in the United States. It is imperative that the Black intellectual unite critique with possibility and strategy. To simply point out the inequities and not project a solution is an exercise Black intellectuals can ill-afford to propagate.

The third and final category of Black intellectual West described is the insurgency model or the Black intellectual as a critical, organic catalyst. In this model, the Black intellectual articulates a new regime of truth that emanates from the everyday experiences including the microaggressions and instances of injustice, marginalization, and systemic dissing that Black folk face every single day. This is the work of the Black intellectual—to look more critically at what West calls the indigenous institutional practices that are demystified and deconstructed through the Black gaze. What is intriguing about this critique is the ways in which the Black intellectuals' thinking often abandons Western canons of hegemonic truth in order to embrace post-Western or trans-Western thought. It no longer sees as sacred the celebrated thinking and philosophy that have undergirded hegemony. The work of this Black intellectual is to upset the status quo. It is intellectual labor with the explicit purpose to resist and to reconstruct society in such a way that notions of racism and sexism and ageism and homophobia and other disdaining attitudes and actions that undergird the many policies and practices, rites and rituals of society are not merely denuded by their place in grounding traditional and contemporary societal mores and behaviors. But an agenda of social action accompanies the revelation and uncovering of minimizing and dismissive practices. The primary goal of the Black intellectual as a critical, organic catalyst is to foment or initiate an insurgency. I like what West says about this. He offers, "The central task of postmodern Black intellectuals is to stimulate, hasten, and enable alternative perceptions and practices by dislodging prevailing discourses and powers." What is so compelling about this model is the fact that, unlike that of the bourgeois or the Black intellectual as humanist, the insurgency model sees our work as not mere labor for credentialing, licensing, promoting and tenuring or a grandiose scheme of self-aggrandizement. The Black intellectual as organic, critical catalyst situates our work in a communal space that sees our academic travail as an instrument of resistance as well as a foundation for collective civil rights action.

I have come to challenge particularly my Black intellectual brothers to release your minds, attitudes, and motivations from simply being celebrated by the powers that be in the academy. Understand that you can teach, serve, publish, and be promoted and tenured while racism, marginalization and heinous societal inequities continue to run rampant. You can be celebrated in the academy while African American young men continue to begin in colleges and universities but fail to persist and ultimately graduate. Does your work matter when another's condition is not made better because of the impact of what you have taught or written? What, then, is the purpose? What is the axiological grounding for our work? What is awaiting the outcomes of our gathering here? To whom does it matter that we are meeting and even going through these series of meetings? I am at the age when every day has to matter. Every word I write or speak must be salient. Every academic practice must have meaning. In fact, my challenge to you and to me is to live a purposive as well as principled and pragmatic academic life. This is a spiritual imperative, and I would like to close my time with you inviting you to engage your spiritual selves to critically self-reflect and to embrace the imperative of purposefully and principally and pragmatically perceiving our academic and intellectual endeavors. My scholarship on critical spirituality will serve as the foundation for the closing portion of my remarks.

Let me begin by offering what I believe to be the three benefits of the spiritual dimension of our lives. I completely understand how some might argue about the existence of the spiritual dimension but I can only quickly offer that, without tapping into our spiritual dimension on a regular basis, many of us would find ourselves in a hopeless, almost depressed malaise because the craziness of the academy, the insanity of society, and the pathology of life itself push us towards an explanation and a resolution that are often not found in the everyday, not found in what we can so easily explain, rationalize, and hypothesize. It cannot be explained through our texts, our qualitative or quantitative analyses. Another interview, case study or t-test will not do the trick to comfort our deep sense of having to forever be in a proving stage, legitimating process and justifying modality. But it can be found in the spiritual space of our lives. There are three purposes of the spiritual dimension.

First, the spiritual dimension provides for us our ontology, as well as our teleology. In other words, the meaning and purpose of our existence are explicated through our spirits. The work that emanates from our intellectual endeavors has meaning and becomes tied to or aligned with a greater purpose as we employ our spirits in this work. The primacy of our existence is clearly highlighted through the revealing of our ontological and teleological foundations of our lives.

Second, our spirits motivate us to embrace connectivity, community, or meaningful relationships with others. It compels us to move beyond the confines of individualistic self-absorption and pushes us to deeply consider the Other and the efficacy of being in relationship with the Other. Third, our spirits inform our sense of what is moral, ethical, and just. I won't take the time to articulate the differences between religion and the concept I have developed, critical spirituality. But suffice it to say that, when an individual subscribes to the tenets of critical spirituality, he or she interrogates the ways in which institutional spaces, like the academy and traditional religion, perpetuate the indignities of racism, classism, ableism and homophobia, among a number of other undemocratic practices.

There are four components of critical spirituality. They are critical self-reflection, deconstructive interpretation, performative creativity, and transformative action. When one grounds one's intellectual labor in critical spirituality, the work is moved from merely attaining the traditional achievements and measurements of success into a more political and socially just realm of academic endeavors. The critically spiritual intellectual has embraced his or her personal predispositions on issues of race, class, gender, ability and other markers of cultural difference and has interrogated just where through the process of socialization these notions have emanated. The critically spiritual intellectual puts the work in a much broader context, one that impacts the social and political spaces in which he/she locates his/her commissioned work. The labor of these intellectuals finds its genesis in a calling of sorts. It is an inescapable compunction to write and teach from a perspective grounded in societal transformation toward democratic practice. The achievement is not merely in being published but in publishing work that challenges the very core of readers, that troubles the genuine selves of those who consume the research in order to bring about radical societal change. We know that we all teach and write and even pose inquiries from a particular conceptual and experiential frame. Deconstructive interpretation allows the intellectual to unearth the origins of those conceptual and experiential frames while, at the same time, juxtaposing those particular positions against a platform of what is socially just, what does not perpetuate marginalization of others, and what predispositions are contrary to the democratic and equitable treatment of all people.

May I offer that to face ourselves in our raw state of unvarnished prejudices, proclivities, and predilections takes courage and preparedness to see the ugliness of the grounding of our actual public practices? Critically spiritual intellectuals see their work as purposeful and principled. The work is tied to a deeper meaning and has, at its core, the righting of the injustices that are the daily regimen for Black and poor people. The work is purposive and pragmatic because it is entrenched in the diurnal lives of those who are marginalized with however a prophetic edge. The prophetic edge is that change is going to take place. The prophetic edge is that institutions that have held people of color and people of no financial means hostage will find themselves either changing or facing their own demise. The pragmatic character of our work contextualizes our teaching and scholarship in a civil rights space where our intellectual labors also become the fodder of our organic or public work as agents for radical societal change. Black intellectuals do not have the luxury to do our work outside of a transformative agenda. Our research inquiries cannot only interest our individual intellectual curiosities but also must provide answers to dilemmas, motivation for revolution, and strategy for societal reconstruction.

Critical spirituality is all about releasing our creativity in a performative way to envision a new possibility and reality. It is the power of reimagination. It asks the intellectual to align her/his intellectual curiosities with a much larger project, that of creating a society where justice and equity are more genuinely practiced. I am certain that I am not fully articulating the dynamic that I hope to leave with you. Our academic labor must be tied to the understanding that what we say as well as what we write has creative ability. We literally are creating a whole new reality through our teaching and scholarship. People embrace what we say and what we write and for us to negate the power and efficacy of these academic practices causes us to completely misunderstand the purpose of our work. People's lives are impacted through our intellectual activity, and it is for this reason that our teaching and scholarship must be intimately linked with the very spiritual notion of creativity, performative creativity. That is not only the envisioning of a different reality, but also the envisioning of the strategies to bring that reality to pass. Our questions must be tied to creating a new reality. They must be spiritually entrepreneurial. Our academic curiosities must be linked to creating, seeing beyond what already exists, and calling forth through our intellectual labor an existence that is not yet present but surely through our transformative action can and will come to pass. Before the critically spiritual intellectual engages the mind, he/she has engaged the spirit that frees him/her to see what has not yet been seen, to speak what has not yet been spoken, and to create what has not yet existed. It is the spiritual enterprise of calling those things that be not as though they were.

As I was writing the conclusion of these remarks in a Baltimore, Maryland hotel, across the street from the hotel was a protest of approximately thirty Black men and women with one or two white men mixed in. The men and women were carrying signs declaring that the Tricon Construction Company does not pay area standard wages and benefits. I put down my pen, left my hotel room, and went to the place of the protest. It would be exceptionally counter-productive for me to share with you what I did at that point. Better for us is for you to determine what should be the next steps for a critically spiritual, organic intellectual. As joggers continued to run by the site unscathed by the chanting and the protesting, as businesses continued to operate, visitors continued to gawk at the gold statue in the center of the cul-de-sac as if nothing was going to interfere with their predetermined occupations, what might be the strategies a critically spiritual, organic, Black academic should take regarding this situation? Should this incident become the substance of an article? Should it provide a case for teaching purposes? Should it be left to serve an academic's needs while the needs of the protesters are left bereft of attention? Just what should a Black intellectual do with this? I leave you to decide but, more importantly, to allow your spirit to guide what should be your next steps.

Thank you for your attention.

Biography

Dr. Michael E. Dantley serves as Miami University's Associate Provost and Associate Vice President for Academic Affairs and is also Professor in the department of Educational Leadership in the School of Education, Health, and Society. Prior to his current position, he served as the Associate Dean for Academic Affairs in the School of Education, Health, and Society. He teaches courses in organizational and leadership theory, ethics and leadership, the principalship, the philosophy of educational leadership, and leadership theory and change. His research focuses on leadership, spirituality and social justice.

Contact Info:

Dr. Michael Dantley
Associate Provost & Associate Vice President for Academic Affairs
Professor, Educational Leadership
208 A Roudebush Hall
Miami University
Oxford, Ohio 45056
Email: dantleme@muohio.edu

The History of Black/Africana Studies and Conflicting Epistemological Paradigms

Ruth Reese
The University of North Carolina at Greensboro

Abstract

This historical research project examines the development, evolution, trends, and diversity of Black/Africana Studies programs, departments, and institutes at Predominately White Institutions (PWIs) of higher education in the context of American social and political history. In particular, the conflicting epistemological paradigms of Black/Africana Studies expressed within academe are investigated. These diverse voices reflect the multifarious life experiences and world views of people of African descent in America, particularly among the progenitors and architects of this academic discipline. By examining the roots and branches of Black/Africana Studies at PWIs, this research will inform the reader of various intellectual and philosophical discourses, which are integral to the controversies within the discipline, and present the rationale for the nomenclature used to describe this field of study.

At Predominately White Institutions (PWIs) of higher education in America, the development and evolution of the academic discipline that studies the history, life, culture, and experiences of people of African descent is the story of the struggle for legitimacy and against marginalization within the academy. The existence of Black/Africana Studies as an academic discipline is often tenuous and periodically under attack. Aldridge and Young (2000) concur by stating that

the tenuousness of acceptability remained the same for the first fifteen years following their introduction.

22

Arguments for the denial, abridgement, or withdrawal of black studies programs extend along a continuum of objectives (p. 5).

Sadly, this struggle is a mirror reflection of its curricula. Harris (2006) adds that "the discipline of Black Studies enjoys the same ambiguous status that Black Americans enjoy" (p. 21).

The nomenclature for this field of study: Afro-American Studies, African American Studies, Africana Studies, Black Studies, Pan African Studies, etc., are often interchangeable, yet reflect the pedagogies and curricula ascribed to diverse schools of thoughts, ideologies, philosophies, and theories which are foundational to each of these various representations.

For the purpose of this study, the researcher will utilize Black/Africana Studies as the chosen descriptor, except when specifically referencing a particular context.

Among these varied epistemological paradigms are traditional academic constructs, oppositional viewpoints, and alternative conceptualizations. Seminal to the variances and subsequent conflicts in theory and ideology that have arisen is a philosophical disagreement over what constitutes the true knowledge base and valid approach to scholarship within the academic discipline of Black/Africana Studies. This schism has produced two notable factions within academe: the integrationist/inclusionist and the Afrocentrist. This research hopes to offer insight into both epistemological paradigms while answering the question: Has the conflict between the integrationist/inclusionist and Afrocentrist approaches to the study of people of African descent in higher education at PWIs affected the academic validity and sustainability of Black/Africana Studies?

This inquiry into the changing roles, divergent missions, and academic goals of Black/Africana Studies may help to quell the need for a "single story" interpretation of the experiences of people of African descent and allow students to embrace the scholarly voice they hear most clearly without fear of intellectual reprimand or cerebral bullying.

Conceptual Framework

The primary research question was developed in a historical/chronological context considering four areas of interest pertaining to the development and evolution of Black/Africana Studies at PWIs of higher education in America. First is a consideration of certain historical events inclusive of intellectual, political, and organizational developments in Black America that transpired from the early eighteenth century to the late twentieth century. Second, which is immersed in the first, is a review of the ideologies and philosophies of the precursors of Black/Africana Studies along with contemporary scholars in the discipline. Third is an investigation of the various epistemological paradigms and nomenclature that developed and evolved over the history of Black/Africana Studies at PWIs. Fourth is a discussion on the scholar activist and the role of that concept in Black/Africana Studies.

This research is intended to provide substance and context to the diverse dimensions of this academic discipline by establishing a frame of reference for the historical problems and need for creating Black/Africana Studies and for describing the relationship between the historical factors and factions.

Roots of Black/Africana Studies

The history of Black/Africana Studies predates the Civil Rights Movement of the 1950s and the turbulent, rebellious 1960s, which was immortalized by Willie Ricks (aka Mukasa Dada), a Civil Rights worker and Field Secretary for the Student Nonviolent Coordinating Committee (SNCC), whose call for "Black Power," a term popularized by Stokely Carmichael (aka Kwame Ture), became a movement. Some scholars contend that Black/Africana Studies began millennia before the African kidnappings referred to as the Trans-Atlantic Slave Trade. Others begin the field of study in the pre-revolutionary war years of the European-American colonies with the arrival in 1565 of Africans in chattel bondage. Irrespective of these perspectives, Conyers, Jr. (1995) defines "Black Studies" as the organizing of knowledge around the experiences of people of African descent. It is both historical and contemporary, since it must deal with the experience itself with its real issues and problems lived in the past and present" (pp. 1-2).

This "knowledge around experiences" acknowledges, validates, and celebrates a people and their contributions long ignored by a universalistic approach to education based on a hegemonic belief system.

Many personalities, scholars, and movements contributed to the field of Black/Africana Studies in American higher education. The intellectual, political, and organizational developments of pre-Civil Rights Black America provide an historical context for the contemporary cultivation, founding, and perpetuation of Black/Africana Studies as an academic discipline in American higher education.

The history of published literature by a person of African descent in America began with Jupiter Hammon and Phyllis Wheatley in the 18th century, who gave expression to their "knowledge around experiences" through poetry. In the 19th century, the Black Abolitionist Movement produced David Walker and his publication of his pamphlet *Walker's Appeal*; Frederick Douglass wrote of his tribulations as he journeyed from slavery to freedom and published the newspaper, the *North Star*; Isabella Baumfree, a former slave, changes her name to Sojourner Truth and begins to preach for the abolition of slavery; and Harriet Tubman escapes slavery and helps other via the Underground Railroad.

After the Civil War, white mob violence against people of African descent in America escalated and continued into the twentieth century. Massacres and lynching were the norm for these paramilitary white supremacist groups as Jim Crow laws replaced the Black Codes. From these real life experiences emerged Ida B. Wells and the Anti-Lynching movement. Most notably joining her crusade was W.E.B. Du Bois, who co-founded the Niagara Movement, which begets the National Negro Committee, precursor to the interracial and interfaith civil rights organization, the National Association for the Advancement of Colored People (NAACP). Shortly afterwards, the National Urban League (NUL), formerly known as the National League on Urban Conditions Among Negroes, is formed. All of these organizations advocated against racial discrimination, sometimes through politics and the judiciary, and other times through the market.

In 1915, Carter G. Woodson founded the Association for the Study of Negro Life and History, which began publishing the *Journal of Negro History* the following year. This was the first academic journal devoted to the study of African American history. In 1926 he proposes Negro History Week. Mary Church Terrell worked in the Women's Suffrage movement, was president of the National Association of Colored Women's Clubs, founded the National Association of College Women, wrote extensively in White and Black newspapers, and was a founding member of the NAACP with Wells and Du Bois. Thurgood Marshall and Charles Hamilton Houston of the NAACP successfully argued two landmark education cases: *Murray v. Pearson* and *Brown v. Board of Education of Topeka, KS.*

All of these African American experiences during the first half of the twentieth century, the subsequent events of the Civil Rights Movement, and the activism of the Black Power Movement sparked in a new generation of African American college students heightened expectations for inclusion in the American Dream, by any means necessary, Thus, Black/Africana Studies was born. L. Redmond and C. P. Henry (2005) remind us that the

> Histories of Black Studies often views its development as emerging from the Black Power Movement with no link to the Civil Rights movement. At worse, they present Civil Rights and Black Power as opposites. Our Analysis links the two movements together as essential to the formation of black studies. (p. 165)

Black Studies in the Academy

The 1950s induced societal changes in America and the demands by African Americans for full citizenship precipitated increased enrollment in the nations' Predominately White Institutions of higher education in the 1960s. Subsequently, these students demanded validation of the contributions of Black people to American history by curricular inclusion at these institutions. Asante (2006) asserts that

"Black Studies" was a term that grew out of the political and academic climate of the 1960s. When students at San Francisco State campaigned in 1968 for courses that reflected the experiences of African people, they called for Black Studies because so much of the curriculum was "White Studies" parading as if it were universal. (p. 317)

Asante (2006), further clarifies his assertion by stating that

The Black Studies movement [arose] from an organized group of ideas that formed a core philosophy for use in confronting the status quo in education. It was unlike any other transformation in the Academy. Groups of students from various colleges, acting simultaneously…passed through the same processes to establish Black Studies on their campuses…the Black Studies movement was a move for self-definition, self-determination, and mental liberation…never before had Black [denoting ethnic and cultural energy] and Studies [intellectual component] been used in the same term. (p. 321)

As the academic discipline changed and evolved, there developed opposing schools of thought regarding the study of people of African descent in America and the Diaspora. The ensuing conflicts have affected the status of Black/Africana Studies at these Predominately White Institutions of higher education.

Conflicts in the Academy over the Study of Black People

During the latter part of the twentieth century as the need to validate the existence of Black/Africana Studies at PWIs was growing, the discipline was also experiencing internal hemorrhaging. Several schisms caused by oppositional viewpoints and alternative conceptualizations were occurring, producing within the academic discipline various nomenclature, ideologies, and theories. Hines (1997) believes that "the ongoing debate over nomenclature is a graphic illustration of residual problems growing out of the turbulent times in which these programs burst upon the academic scene" (p. 7).

The politically charged 1960s forced many institutions of higher education in America to find a home in the academy for Black/Africana Studies. Questions of legitimacy, worth and appropriateness existed from the beginning. Often the discipline became defined by issues surrounding definition and identity. This is reflected in the diversity of names used to designate the field of study and has contributed to the various levels of fragmentation in missions, theoretical frameworks, goals, and curricula. Butler (2000) argues that the Du Boisian Identification of African American double consciousness is the springboard for much discussion and policy making about African Americans. The institutional and structural development of African American studies derived its guiding principles, structures, methodologies, and approaches from various interpretations of or responses to his constructs. The degree of liberatory and agentive impotence in conceptualizations and formulations of African American studies at the dawn of the twenty-first century emanate to some extent from contemporary characteristics of higher education and that, moreover, the particular positioning of African American studies in assimilationists, diasporic, pluralistic, and Afrocentric camps all reflect, to lesser or greater degrees, the failure of African American scholars and administrators to engage from shared and related perspectives the ambivalences, ambiguities, and regimes of truth maintained by the self/other binary that Du Bois urged us to address in 1903 (p. 142).

In the appendix (pp.421-432) to their *Handbook of Black Studies* in a section titled "The Unsettled Discourse," Molefi Asante and Maulana Karenga (2006) identify 246 programs and departments that deal with some aspect of the study of people of Africa and African descent within the Diaspora. The names utilized in representing the discipline include African Studies (41), African and African Diaspora (1), African/Black World Studies (2), Pan African Studies (5), Africology (1), Africa and New World Studies (1), African, African American, and Caribbean Studies (1); African Studies (13); African New World Studies (1); Black World Studies (1); Latin American Studies (4), Latin American and Caribbean Studies (6); Black and Hispanic Studies (1), Africana and Latin American Studies (1); African and African American Studies (31); African American Studies (73); Afro-American Studies (10); African American Education Program (1); Afro-Ethnic Studies (1); American Ethnic Studies (2); American Studies–African-American Emphasis (1); Black Studies (34); Comparative American Cultures (1); Ethnic Studies Programs (12); Race and Ethnic Studies (1); and 30 specialized programs, including various Institutes, Africana Studies Archives and African Language Programs.

Clearly, there must be some overlapping and confusion regarding variations in curricular content with no standardization in design. Can this mean that among the major academicians in this field of study the conflicts are less noteworthy than the literature portends? Ama Mazama, a radical and unapologetic Africocentrist, as quoted in Hall (1999), views the "multiplicity of paradigms or schools of thought within Africana Studies...[as] necessary and positive" (p. 11). Possibly, as Rabaka (2006) suggests that

> Disciplinary development is predicated on discursive formations to which Africana Studies—that is, Africana, Pan-African, African American, and Black Studies—is not immune. Discursive formations, meaning essentially knowledge production and dissemination,

> what we would call in Africana Studies "epistemologies" or "theories of knowledge," provide the theoretical thrust(s) that help to guide and establish interdisciplinary arenas while simultaneously exploding traditional disciplinary boundaries. (p. 131)

Or might it be that the more honest portrayal of the clash between the traditional integrationists/inclusionist world view and the Afrocentric world view in program design, construct, and theory undergirds unyielding regimes of truth incapable of acknowledging diversity of experiences and perspectives among people of African descent in America? This "oppositional consciousness" (p. 182) as described by Redmond and Henry (2005) in itself offers proof that even the theoretical worlds of academe are not resistant to real life issues and experiences. Remembering the concept of "knowledge around experience," Turner (2000) argues that

> The theoreticians of black studies use the basic social science concept of the sociology of knowledge to explain the legitimacy of the idea that the position of black people in the social structure not only offers peculiar insights, but also represents a specific meaning about societal truth. Furthermore, all knowledge is a perspective on shared experience. (p. 65)

Fortunately, all perspectives recognize the role of student activism in the sustainability of Black/Africana Studies.

The Scholar Activist

It is commonly acknowledged and well-documented that the student activism of the 1950s, 60s, and 70s was an integral constituent in the Civil Rights and Black Power Movements, and definitively the fuel for the fire in the demand and creation of Black/African Studies at PWIs. Student activism was a core component in the early days of the discipline, "where a deep commitment to human liberation and constant social transformation" (Rabaka, 2006, p. 133) was axiomatic to the era. Students believed in the potential liberatory nature of higher education while experiencing suppression and rage at the obvious inequalities of American society.

In 1968, influenced by the Civil Rights movements, the African Heritage Studies Association (AHSA), "a national organization of 'scholar activist'" (p. 51) cites Morgan-Cato (2006), formed with John Henrik Clark as a founding member. It focused, states Morgan-Cato, on "Black academic leadership in research, interpretation, and development. It claimed leadership in the Pan-Africanist Black Studies movement and provided many of the staff for the first wave of Black Studies efforts in Northern Colleges" (p. 53). According to Mazama (2006)

> Africana Studies students were supposed to learn, as part of their training to commit themselves to the betterment of their community and to become "scholar-activist." However, the process of professionalization, which requires Africana Studies...students to devote their energies to academic work....may have been detrimental to social activism and the fulfilling of the initial mission of Africana Studies. (p. 9)

Unfortunately, Kershaw (2003) reminds us, referencing Carter G. Woodson and his classic volume, the *Mis-education of the Negro*:

> that the education of the "Negro" takes him away from solving the needs of the people to pursuits of individual self-aggrandizement. African American people want an education that helps them to solve problems (pp 27-28).

There was concern in the literature that the epistemological conflicts not only affect the viability of Black Studies as an academic discipline, but these conflicts also help to support the rupture between scholarship and activism, which was initially an intentional consideration in the founding of the discipline. Although the literature did voice distress with the inherent variance in diverse epistemological paradigms, it also expressed great admiration for the concept of scholar activist and unanimously place it central to the mission and sustainability of Black/African Studies at PWIs. As Black/Africana Studies reclaims the scholar activist, it is also setting agendas for new research on many contemporary issues.

Trends

The future, as in the past, of Black/Africana Studies is about multitudinous experiences of diverse people of African descent in America and throughout the Diaspora. For fifty years, Black/Africana American Studies has ebbed and flowed with the tides of popularity and disfavor. Energized by the current bank of research scholars in the discipline, Black/Africana Studies is branching out from the narrow confines of simply historical and sociological analyses, to defining and exploring original areas of scholarship needed to keep the field of study vibrant, relevant, and sustained. "African-American/Black Studies," contend Aldridge and Young (2000), "holds the potential to expand the dimensions of knowledge, explore uncharted areas of research, attract and reach an untapped pool of students, and provide the society with trained professionals who contribute to the positive growth and development of their communities" (p. 5).

Conclusion

Born out of the intellectual, political, economic, and social collisions of the African experience in America and throughout the Diaspora, the academic discipline of Black/Africana Studies has sought to express, according to Harris (2006), the existence of "an unique and identifiable African worldview...and...that world view is the foundation for best practices in all walks of African American life" (p. 16). Du Bois and Woodson's charge to literate African Americans to implement an enduring foundation for the study of People of African descent at institutions of higher education, came to fruition in the late 60s and early 70s as Predominately White Institutions acquiesced to the demands of its Black students who voiced the desire have their history told without apology, distortion, or malfeasance. As Reviere (2006) recounts

> The skewed power relations that have resulted from the past 500 years of European and African contact have resulted in a one-dimensional perspective of the human story. Eurocentrist have continuously assumed the right to tell their own stories and everyone else's—and from a solely one-dimensional perspective. This has meant that the resulting Eurocentric stories are always incomplete and often distorted and consequently untrue. (p. 265)

This non-European worldview proposed by Black/Africana Studies posed ideological and philosophical challenges to traditional White institutions of higher education that circumvented over time the agreements to the demands by institutionally devaluing the discipline with insufficient faculty and resources.

Consequently, the problems facing Black/Africana Studies became both external and internal. Christian (2006) states that Black/Africana Studies

> has developed to become a field of study that has multiple perspectives. One could argue that this is a positive thing for Black Studies not to be a homogenous discipline....but with Black Studies being divergent in philosophy, it... [has] caused indirect stagnation" (p. 80).

However, as the discipline matures, these factions are coexisting in professional organizations, such as the National Council of Black Studies that is dedicated to promoting academic excellence and social responsibility. Therefore, as the scholar activist reclaims his/her rightful place as core to the mission of Black/Africana Studies, hopefully the discipline will move from the margins and resist through scholarship any external and internal qualms regarding legitimacy and worth as it matures past its journey of fifty years. Obviously there are more threads to follow in this research, and more concerns and issues. For future research scholars can explore the integration of these opposing epistemological paradigms within the professional organizations that support the diversity of the scholarship.

Bibliography

Aldridge, D. P., & Young, C. (Eds.). (2000). *Out of the revolution: The development of Africana studies.* Lanham, MD: Lexington Books.

Asante, M. K. (2006). The pursuit of Africology: On the creation and sustaining of Black studies. In M. K. Asante & M. Karenga, (Eds.). *Handbook of Black Studies.* Thousand Oaks, CA: SAGE Publications.

Asante, M. K., & Karenga, M. (Eds.) (2006). *Handbook of Black Studies.* Thousand Oaks, CA: SAGE Publications.

Butler, J. E. (2000). African American studies in the "warring ideals." In M. Marable (Ed.). *Dispatches from the ebony tower: Intellectuals confront the African American experience.* New York, NY: Columbia University Press.

Christian, M. (2006). Philosophy and practice for Black studies: The case of researching White supremacy. In M. K. Asante & M. Karenga, (Eds.). *Handbook of Black Studies.* Thousand Oaks, CA: SAGE Publications.

Conyers, J. L., Jr. (1995). The evolution of African American studies: A descriptive and evaluative analysis of selected African American studies departments and programs. Lanham, MD: University Press of America, Inc.

Conyers, J. L., Jr. (Ed.). (1997). *Africana studies: A disciplinary quest for both theory and method.* Jefferson, NC: McFarland & Company, Inc., Publishers.

Conyers, J. L., Jr. (Ed.). (2003). *Afrocentricity and the academy: Essays on theory and practice.* Jefferson, NC: McFarland & Company, Inc., Publishers.

Conyers, J. L., Jr. (Ed.). (2005). *Afrocentric traditions.* New Brunswick, NJ: Transaction Publishers.

Gordon, L. R., & Gordon, J. A. (Eds.). (2006). *A companion to African-American studies.* Malden, MA: Blackwell Publishing.

Hall, P. A. (1999). *In the vineyard: Working in African American studies.* Knoxville, TN: The University of Tennessee Press.

Harris, N. (2006). Black to the future: Black studies and network Nommo. In M. K. Asante & M. Karenga. (Eds.). *Handbook of Black Studies.* Thousand Oaks, CA: SAGE Publications.

Hines, D. C. (1997). Black studies: An overview. In J. L. Conyers, (Ed.). *Africana studies: A disciplinary quest for both theory and method.* Jefferson, NC: McFarland & Company, Inc., Publishers.

Kershaw, T. (2003). The Black studies paradigm: The making of scholar activist. In J. L. Conyers, Jr. (Ed.). (2003) *Afrocentricity and the academy: Essays on theory and practice.* Jefferson, NC: McFarland & Company, Inc., Publishers.

Marable, M. (Ed.). (2000). *Dispatches from the ebony tower: Intellectuals confront the African American experience.* New York, NY: Columbia University Press.

Morgan-Cato, C. (2006). Black studies in the whirlwind: A retrospective view. In L. R. Gordon & J. A. Gordon. (Eds.). *A companion to African-American studies.* Malden, MA: Blackwell Publishing.

Rabaka, R. (2006). African critical theory of contemporary society: The role of radical politics, social theory and Africana philosophy. In M. K. Asante & M. Karenga, (Eds.). *Handbook of Black Studies.* Thousand Oaks, CA: SAGE Publications.

Redmond, L. & Henry, C. P. (2005). The roots of Black studies. In J. L. Conyers, Jr. *Afrocentric traditions.* New Brunswick, NJ: Transaction Publishers.

Reviere, R. (2006). The cannons of Afrocentric research. In M. K. Asante & M. Karenga, (Eds.). *Handbook of Black Studies.* Thousand Oaks, CA: SAGE Publications.

Turner, J. (2000). Africana studies and epistemology. In D. P. Aldridge C. & Young, C. (Eds.). *Out of the revolution: The development of Africana studies.* Lanham, MD: Lexington Books.

Biography

In addition to serving as graduate research assistant to Dr. C.P. Gause, employed as an instructor in the University's Student Academic Success Program, and recently was accepted and joined the 2011 Cohort of the Summerbridge Breakthrough Alumni Network (SBAN) Teacher of Color Preparatory Institute (TCPI).

Middle School to High School Transition of African American Males: A Closer Look

Anissia Jenkins Scales
University of North Carolina, Greensboro

Over the years, there has been a decline in student achievement during the middle to high school transition period (Forgan & Vaughn, 2000; Somers, Owens, & Piliawsky, 2009). More specifically, while the transition from middle school to high school is difficult for many students, African American males are more significantly affected during this crucial transition (Bailey & Paisley, 2004; Graham, Taylor, & Hudley, 1998). In fact, according to Pluviose (2008), fewer than 50% of African American males graduate from high school. The transition from middle school to high school has been noted as one roadblock to high school graduation for African American males (Somers et al., 2009).

Dropout research indicates that students, especially African American males, tend to drop out of high school either during or shortly after the ninth grade (Hymel, Comfort, Schonert-Reichl, & McDougall, 1996; Smith 1997; Somers et al., 2009; Wyatt, 2009). This dropout rate for African American males has more serious ramifications in that it "only feeds the violent crime rate; in some cases eighty percent of the state prison population is African American males" (Pluviose, 2008, p. 5). These statistics are alarming. Dropout prevention research and programs are critical because the costs socially and monetarily are great for American society if such programs are not instituted. It is estimated that the monetary costs for students who drop out of high school range into billions of dollars (Somers et al., 2009). Taken together, these staggering statistics should act as a catalyst for researchers to examine more closely why African American males are dropping out of high school.

Although there have been several studies conducted on transition programs and interventions (e.g., Cauley & Jovanovich, 2006; Lindsay, 1997; McIntosh & White, 2006; Potter, Schlisky, Stevenson, & Drawdy, 2001), the actual evidence and results of implementation are scarce in schools with a high population of transitioning African American males. If the schools do not implement the effective transition interventions/strategies that are needed, these students will be in immediate peril. Researchers found that "academic failure during the transition to high school is directly linked to the probability of dropping out [of high school]" (Cauley & Jovanovich, 2006, p. 32).

Most middle schools and high schools are eager to find a remedy or at least develop a plan that will help their students successfully get through this difficult period (McIntosh & White, 2006). Early research studies (Alspaugh, 1998; Eccles, Lord, & Midgely, 1991) focused on overall or general student transition. As time and research have progressed, researchers have identified successful transition strategies (Capstick, 2008; Cauley & Jovanovich, 2006; Cushman, 2006; Mizelle, 2005) and there has been a shift in conducting more research studies on middle school/high school transition through the lens of gender, race/ethnicity, and socioeconomic status (Heck & Mahoe, 2006). Although the lens of researchers may be shifting, it is important to recognize that there remains a gap in the transition literature with regard to African American males and how they perceive they are affected during the transition to high school.

The literature on middle school to high school transition names three main aspects that affect student transition: the structural domain, the academic domain, and the personal domain (Cauley & Jovanovich, 2006; Chmelynski, 2003). Within each domain are several factors that contribute to successful or unsuccessful transitions to high school. The structural domain contains the physical environment, discipline procedures, and the absence of teaming. The academic domain includes curricular issues, teacher/school expectations, and student attendance. Last, the personal domain consists of social interactions, motivation, and identity. One drawback of the transition literature is most of the transition research speaks to academic factors—curricular issues, teacher/school expectations, and attendance (Capstick 2008; Cauley & Jovanovich, 2006; Heller, Calderon, & Medrich, 2003) and structural factors—physical environment, discipline procedures, and the absence of teaming (McIntosh & White, 2006; Morgan & Hertzog, 2001)—affecting successful transitions for students from the perspectives of the researchers (as opposed to the perspectives of the students themselves). Another deficiency in the literature lies in examining personal factors affecting successful transitions for African American males. Currently, there is not a wealth of knowledge in the area of middle school to high school transition and successful transition facilitators for African American males. The need for more effective strategies and interventions to help African American males successfully transition to high school initiated my study.

The theoretical perspective that informed my inquiry regarding successful transition of African American males from middle school to high school was critical race theory (CRT). Critical Race Theory is the lens being used to view the transition of African American males from middle school to high school because it speaks to the power and oppression of structural institutions like schools. It also looks at the intersections of race and gender. CRT fosters an understanding of hegemony in American education. Gause (2008) goes further to explain that "the educational process in which African American children engage is hegemonic at its best and catastrophic at its worst and it reflects European cultural and educative hegemony" (p. 70).

According to Sleeter and Bernal (2003), critical race theory was "developed to address social justice and racial oppression in U.S. society and speaks to the barriers of oppression such as racism, classism, etc. in institutions like schools" (p. 247). In a historic sense, the CRT perspective originated with two legal scholars, Derrick Bell and Alan Freeman, who had become discontented with the slow pace of racial reform in the United States. In their definitive work, *Toward a Critical Race Theory of Education*, Gloria Ladson-Billings and William Tate (1995) adapted CRT to educational research and practice. There are four tenets of CRT: counterstorytelling, permanence of race, interest convergence, and social construction of race—challenge to dominant society. I have focused on three of the tenets: (a) counterstorytelling, (b) racism is normal, ordinary in American society, and (c) the concept of interest convergence—when a society's elites allow or encourage advances by a subordinated group only when such advances also promote the self-interest of the elites (Sleeter & Bernal, 2003). I am focusing on these three tenets because they provide support for the lens I am using in my study. These tenets also align nicely with the three domains of factors affecting middle school to high school transition: structural, academic, and personal.

The purpose of this modified explanatory mixed methods study was to examine structural, academic, and personal factors affecting the transition of African American males to high school by giving voice to the participants.

Methodology

The justification for the modified explanatory mixed methods approach is that it makes the study more valid and complete in that the qualitative data (from phase two of data analysis) is used to further examine and understand the quantitative findings (from phase one of data analysis). The first phase of data collection in this study was a questionnaire. The second phase of data collection was individual interviews and a focus group interview. Although I collected the quantitative data first, more emphasis was placed on the qualitative data (Creswell, 2005). Therefore, I rely heavily on the qualitative data to explain themes and conclusions that emerged from the data analysis.

The modified explanatory mixed methods design is most appropriate for this study because using a quantitative or qualitative methodology alone would not tell the entire story of successful middle school to high school transition. Using this approach, I will be able to better understand the participants' perceptions of their transition experiences, quantitatively and qualitatively. Looking at both quantitative and qualitative data will ensure a more comprehensive and inclusive study.

Context of the Study

Meadowview High School was chosen as the study site because it has a large population of African American males in the ninth grade. Meadowview has four grade levels: ninth, tenth, eleventh, and twelfth grades. Of the 1431 students, 394 students are African American males spanning over grades 9, 10, 11, and 12. There are 128 African American males in the ninth grade. Meadowview is on a 4-period block schedule with classes meeting for ninety (90) minutes daily. The school environment is inviting: hallways are well-lit, staff members are friendly, and there are samples of student work at the entrance, and the faculty and staff aim for the students to do well academically through the accomplishment of short-term and long-term goals.

For many years, Meadowview High School had carried a reputation of academic excellence and high athletic distinction. In each graduating class, Meadowview High had over half of its graduates who were leaving to attend reputable colleges/universities, trade schools, and technical institutions. Additionally, the athletic program at Meadowview High School was ranked very high in the district.

Within the last ten years, there has been a change in the level of academics at the high school. According to the state assessment data, the academic achievement levels of Meadowview have declined. There are many theories for why the change in academic achievement has occurred. Some attribute the decline to shifting demographics and the prevalence of gang activity within the school. Others attribute the academic deterioration to the lack of student and parent accountability. Yet, some believe that the decline in academic success is due to teacher preparation and accountability.

In response to the downward spiral of academic achievement, Meadowview High added a new component to the academic structure of the school. It acquired magnet school status. The magnet program focused on the International Baccalaureate (IB) Diploma Programme. The IB program was instituted in an attempt to attract and retain students who would take advantage of the opportunities the program provided. In addition, the IB program was designed in part to raise the academic expectations of teachers, students, and parents. The IB

Diploma Programme takes place during the eleventh and twelfth grades, with ninth- and tenth-grade courses providing the foundations necessary for success in the program. The rigorous course of study provides a liberal arts curriculum from a global perspective with university-level work and required examinations that are developed and marked on an international standard (school website).

Participants

The participants in this study are ninth-grade African American males. They attend the same urban school, Meadowview High School, in the southeastern region of the United States. This group was targeted for this study because unlike the tenth, eleventh, and twelfth graders, they have recently experienced the transition from middle school to high school.

The ages of all participants (quantitative and qualitative phases) ranged from 14 to 16 years old. After viewing progress reports and attendance records of each participant, two students were considered above average academically (3.0 or higher), four students were average (2.0 to 2.9), and two students experienced difficulty (1.9 and below) in academic courses.

Data Collection

Because this is a modified explanatory mixed methods study, data was collected in two phases: quantitative and qualitative. During the first phase of data collection, the data source used was a questionnaire. The questionnaire contained item responses ranging from strongly agree to strongly disagree. In phase two, data was collected using (a) two individual interviews; (b) one focus group interview; and (c) notes from the researcher's journal. Interview protocols were created for the individual interview and the focus group interview. All data were collected between January 2009 and June 2009.

The questionnaire consisted of twenty-eight items. Every effort was made to keep the number of questions to a minimum because of the population that was being surveyed. Lengthy questionnaires may result in apathy and frustration for the participants (Gall, Borg, & Gall, 1996). Continuous scaled data was used and the item responses ranged from strongly agree to strongly disagree.

In the qualitative phase of data collection, several data sources were used. The sources included two individual interviews per participant and one focus group interview, a researcher's journal, and archival data, which included academic, attendance, and discipline records.

Data Analysis

Similar to data collection, data analysis was also carried out in two phases: quantitative and qualitative. The quantitative analysis was completed by using descriptive statistics and inferential statistics. The qualitative analysis included coding the data from each individual interview and the focus group interview and identifying and interpreting overall emerging themes.

Findings

The response choices were based on a four-point Likert scale with ratings ranging from 1=strongly disagree (SD) to 4=strongly agree (SA). The questionnaire included three subscales: structural, academic, and personal. Since all of the participants were African American males who had completed the first semester of ninth grade, only one demographic variable was included on the questionnaire: age.

Quantitative Results

Descriptive Statistics

The structural subscale consisted of nine items. There were three categories of the structural factors: three items addressing how the respondents felt about the size of the school, three items addressing how they felt about the discipline procedures of the school, and three items measuring how the respondents felt about the absence of interdisciplinary teaming. The grand mean score for the structural factors subscale was 2.37 with standard deviation scores ranging from .458 to .976.

The academic factors subscale also consisted of nine items. Three categories assessed the academic factors subscale: three items measured how the respondents felt about teacher expectations, four items focused on how they felt about the academic demands of high school, and two items assessed how respondents felt about course requirements. The grand mean of the academic subscale was 2.63 with standard deviation scores ranging from .426 to 1.019.

There were ten items within the personal factors subscale. The personal factors were assessed by three categories: four items assessed how the respondents felt about relationships with teachers, three items measured how they felt about their relationships with friends, and three items assessed how they felt about their relationships with family/community members. The grand mean score of the personal subscale was 2.76 with standard deviation scores ranging from .594 to .884.

Inferential Statistics

Since this was not a quantitative dominant study, only two inferential statistics were applied: Cronbach's alpha to establish reliability and an independent *t*-test to examine differences between the two age groups.

Cronbach's alpha is a measure of internal consistency or how closely related a set of items is as a group (Creswell, 2005). In this study, Cronbach's alpha was used to examine the reliability (internal consistency) of the structural, academic, and personal subscales. The reliability of the structural subscale was .621, the academic subscale was .568, and the personal factors subscale was .851. The internal consistency of the questionnaire overall was .892. According to Garson (2002), "the widely-accepted social science cut-off is that alpha should be .70 or higher for a set of items to be considered a scale, but some use .75 or .80 while others are as lenient as .60" (p. 189).

Consequently, the overall questionnaire and personal subscale were highly reliable. The structural subscale had an acceptable level of reliability, but internal consistency for the academic subscale was a little weak.

There was a wide age range among the ninth grade participants. Therefore, an independent *t*-test was performed in order to compare the manner in which 16-year-olds and 14-year-olds responded to the questionnaire. In this study, there were two 16-year-olds and thirteen 14-year-olds. Both age groups answered most of the questionnaire items similarly. However, the *t*-test revealed there were four items where responses were significantly different: two items in the academic domain and two items in the personal domain.

Qualitative Results

Qualitative data were analyzed using Creswell's (2008) content analysis coding procedures. Eight themes related to structural, academic, and personal factors emerged: (a) School Size Is Not A Problem, But … (physical structure); (b) Hangin' With My Friends In Class: Missing the Interdisciplinary Team Structure (academic structure); (c) Teachers Think We Can't Do the Work (teacher expectations); (d) This Is Harder Than I Thought It Would Be (academic expectations and academic assistance); (e) My Friends Save Me: Camaraderie of the "Brothers" at School (relationships with peers); (f) Teachers: Friend or Foe? (relationships with teachers); (g) You're Not There to Take Up Space: Great Expectations of Parents/Guardians and Community (home and community relationships); and (h) Plight of the Young Black Male—The Saga Continues (sociopsychological issues).

Conclusions

The conclusions and findings from analysis of the data are aligned with the research questions, in correspondence with the research literature.

What do ninth-grade African American males describe as structural, academic, and personal barriers related to their transition?

The participants in this study did not think there were major structural barriers to a successful middle school to high school transition. Although the participants agreed that, initially, when they (and other students) moved to high school, the size of the building and its newness was intimidating, as time passed, students became more comfortable and familiar with the size; therefore, the structure of the school was not such an issue anymore. In fact, the participants stated the problems with the school building structure ended within days of the start of school, which is the reason individually and collectively they did not consider the physical structure of Meadowview a barrier to a successful high school transition. While school size may not have been a barrier, it was revealed that overcrowding was an issue for these participants. In addition to physical school size, the participants also offered an explanation for why they thought the teaming process was important (for organizational purposes) in middle school and, conversely, why, in high school, the teaming concept may not be as necessary. Some participants initially stated they missed the middle school teams but others admitted they preferred the manner in which high school classes were arranged. They enjoyed the freedom that departmentalization offered. As a result of the short-lived experiences of unfamiliarity (school building) and adjustment (departmentalization), the physical structure and the academic structure (absence of teaming, move to departmentalization) of the high school were not considered major barriers to a successful middle school to high school transition for these participants.

The idea of structural factors was not a major barrier to a successful middle school to high school transition is inconsistent with the research literature on the topic. According to the research literature, the physical change of the school structure is extremely difficult for adolescents as they move from middle school to high school (Brenner & Graham, 2009; Cushman, 2006; Isakson & Jarvis, 1999; Mizelle 2005). The responsibility of navigating through this new environment may be a cause of stress and uneasiness for the students (Lindsay, 1997; Chapman & Sawyer, 2001). Additionally, students tend to feel isolated and lonely in their new high schools as a result of the school size (Chapman & Sawyer, 2001).

The change can overwhelm the coping skills of some students, lower self esteem, and decrease motivation to learn. For some students, the singular and unsettling act of changing from one school in eighth grade to a new school in high school may be a precipitating factor in dropping out" (Letrello & Miles, 2003, p. 213).

For the participants in this study, the change in structure from middle school to high school was not a barrier to their transitions. However, it is important to note that, while the participants came to the conclusion that, for their individual transition experiences, the structure of high school did not present a roadblock, each participant recognized and identified the disorientation he felt when he arrived on Meadowview's campus for the first time. The researcher's conclusion is that the change in school structure presented a barrier to high school transition for these participants, as the research literature posits; however, a transition facilitator, rather it was a teacher or friend, helped to reduce the anxiety and apprehension caused by the change in school size, location of classes, and the new academic structure, thus assisting them in overcoming the structural transition barriers.

In this study, the participants felt there were specific academic barriers to a successful middle school to high school transition. The academic barriers included: (a) change in teacher expectations and (b) rigor of academic assignments and coursework. Although seven out of eight of the participants knew that the level of coursework in high school would be different and more difficult than middle school coursework, none of them expected the changes in teacher expectations and the level of academic rigor they received at Meadowview High School. Five out of eight participants felt their middle school classes/classwork did not do an adequate job in preparing them for what they faced in high school. The high school teachers expected the participants (and other students) to be relatively intrinsically motivated and organized. In addition, the participants expressed that it was an expectation that they possess time management skills. The participants recalled receiving assignment after assignment with no way of "really" keeping track of the work. Time management, according to the participants, was not a skill that they learned in middle school because of the teaming process. In middle school, the participants were only responsible for one (or, at most, two) major assignment, project, or test at a time, whereas, in high school, major projects and tests are due more frequently and simultaneously.

The participants reflected on the first semester. They felt time management was a major barrier to a successful middle school to high school transition. They noted, if students do not get a handle on their workload immediately and make a schedule to organize and prioritize assignments, they will fall farther behind and, once students get too far behind in their work, it is almost impossible to regain ground in the classes. The participants also reflected on the change in teacher expectations and the academic rigor. They stated that, while there were a few assignments that required group work, for the most part, the teacher expected them to do more of the work individually. For these participants, working individually meant more accountability and more distress.

The perceptions of the participants are in agreement with the research literature. The academic expectations of high school teachers are different from those of middle school teachers (Mizelle 2005; Morgan & Hertzog, 2001). High school teachers expect their students to think independently and attack assignments using higher level thinking skills, as well as to be astute problem-solvers (Morgan & Hertzog, 2001). This assertion is not to say that middle school teachers do not have high expectations for their students; however, they take a different approach to fostering the needed academic skills. When students arrive at high school, many of them are not accustomed to the level of independent work or the level of rigorous assignments (Jarvis, 1999, Letrello & Miles, 2003; Mizelle, 2005). The participants in this study agreed with the research literature. They found the academic expectations of teachers and the rigor of classes and coursework to be a major barrier to a successful high school transition. The researcher concludes that the change in teacher expectations and academic rigor were major barriers to a successful high school transition for these participants. Similar to the structural aspect, transition facilitators were employed to assist the participants in surmounting the academic barriers.

The participants in this study described several personal barriers to a successful high school transition. According to the participants, the personal barriers affecting their transitions to high school were interpersonal relationships and coping with the racial and gender dilemmas within the context of school.

Interpersonal relationships affecting the high school transition for these participants were divided into two categories: (a) relationships with peers and (b) relationships with adults. The relationships with peers were important to seven out eight of the participants. The participants felt that having their friends at school with them had a large impact on their lives at school. Their friends helped them with academics and they partook in the shared experience of being African American and male at Meadowview High School. There were instances and events that the participants stated they could only share with their friends because they were the only people who would understand the situations they have gone through on a daily basis. The friendships the participants have fostered were both old friendships that have carried over from middle school and newly developed friendships that were formed in school. Without the friendships/relationships with their peers, it seemed to the participants they would not have transitioned successfully to high school. In addition to relationships with peers, relationships with adults—teachers and parents—were important, according to the participants.

Relationships with teachers, to the majority of participants, were essential to a successful transition. Cultivating a positive relationship with teachers can be a benefit for students. The participants mentioned the benefits of having a respectable and pleasant relationship with teachers. They stated that teachers would be more apt to help students with whom they have built a favorable relationship. Additionally, participants felt that teachers who built positive relationships with students made it a point to find out more about their students than their grades, conduct, and extracurricular activities; teachers who are genuinely interested in their students investigate to discover the hobbies of their students outside of academics. It seemed to the participants that middle school teachers were automatically interested in knowing everything about their students. But, when the students got to high school, there were only a few teachers who were interested in their students to the degree of the middle school teachers. Participants in this study also commented on the relationships and expectations of their family/community leaders. The relationships the participants mentioned were relationships with their parents/guardians and their pastors (two participants). The participants understood the expectations of their parents/guardians and community leaders. All of the participants resolved to achieve academically and graduate from high school. They wanted to achieve for their families and community, but they also wanted to achieve for themselves.

The last personal barrier related to transition was coping with the racial and gender dilemmas within the context of school. The participants shared their feelings about the manner in which African American boys are viewed at Meadowview High School. They recalled several instances where they felt they were being treated negatively because they were African American males.

The participants shared that discipline issues were also a part of the personal barrier (racial and gender dilemmas). The young men commented on instances where they were accused of participating in misbehaviors or rule infractions because they were in close proximity to those who committed the actual infractions. The participants felt they were unfairly targeted because they were African American males. In addition, the young men communicated that it seemed as if adults in the building (teachers and administrators) automatically assumed they were involved in wrongdoing. In some cases, not only was the negative assumption made, but the participants also received reprimands and other consequences.

The insights of the participants were in accordance with the research literature. According to Forgan and Vaughn (2000), students have difficulty with high school transition because of the change in interpersonal relationships. Students who move from middle school to high school with their friends are more likely to perform better and have better attendance in high school than those students who do not (Heller et al., 2003). Having an intact social network or developing a social network helps students increase their feelings of belonging. Interpersonal relationships help to combat the loneliness and isolation that may be experienced by adolescents during the transition period (Hymel et al., 1996). Interpersonal relationships with teachers change in that high school teachers tend to be more content-centered and middle school teachers, as a result of the middle school philosophy, was more student-centered (Heck & Mahoe, 2006).

Relationships with parents/family may change as students strive for independence. In addition to striving for independence, students are also forming their own identity (Gause, 2008; Letrello & Miles, 2003). Identity development is difficult for adolescence in general. This process is particularly difficult for African American males because of the negative images that are displayed in society and in schools (Gause, 2008). The researcher concluded the assertions of the study were reflected in the literature on the topic. The personal barriers, interpersonal relationships, and racial and gender dilemmas within the context of the school were barriers related to transition for these participants.

What do ninth-grade African American males describe as structural, academic, and personal facilitators of their transition?

The participants in this study reported transition facilitators for the three aspects: structural, academic, and personal. Although the participants did not identify school structure as a barrier to a successful transition to high school, within their conversations, one could infer that teachers (adults) and the participants' peers were used as facilitators for learning and becoming comfortable with the school building. Furthermore, human resources were also employed as facilitators for the academic aspect. The participants conveyed that they used their teachers and tutors to assist them with their assignments. The tutors were especially helpful in that they facilitated new ways of approaching the subject matter the participants were struggling to successfully complete. The tutors worked with the participants several days a week. In addition, the teachers also worked with the participants one-on-one either after or before school. The participants enjoyed having the opportunity to get more individual or small group assistance. Last, participants reported that personal facilitators for their transitions included new friendships and expectation awareness.

New friendships were identified as a transition facilitator because the participants felt there were fractures in their previous friendships from middle school. New friendships served as a means for coping with the loss or transformation of their friendship networks. Furthermore, the participants noted, being aware of the expectations of parents/guardians and community leaders helped them to make sense of and take responsibility for their actions. In other words, knowing that their parents/guardians and community leaders expected them to do well academically in school helped shape and determine the actions the participants made while they were in school. None of the participants wanted to disappoint their parents/guardians or community leaders. Living up to what was expected of them was a way to avoid disappointing those they cared about most.

How do ninth-grade African American males explain the impact of these barriers and facilitators on their transitions?

According to the participants, the barriers and facilitators had a major impact on their transitions from middle school to high school. Although the participants had anticipated differences in middle school and high school, they had not prepared themselves to handle the extent of the academic and personal barriers they faced. They expressed they wished someone would have explained to them before they actually became ninth grade students what the barriers were and identified facilitators of these barriers prior to the transition. The participants felt that, if they had had some exposure to the barriers and facilitators, they would have had a chance to plan how they wanted to manage their ninth-grade year.

The transition literature speaks to exposing students as eighth graders to high school procedures, expectations, and events (Isakson & Jarvis, 1999); however, the literature does not direct educators to explain to students the barriers and facilitators to middle school to high school transition. Certainly, there is an implicit message to admonish students about the pitfalls of high school but, according to the participants in this study, they would have appreciated and preferred an overview of the specific barriers and facilitators at an open house session or freshman orientation. The researcher agrees with the participants. The barriers and facilitators of transition need to be shared with students and parents prior to the beginning of the students' ninth-grade year. These conversations about the differences between middle school and high school need to begin with the eighth-grade teachers and should go beyond "in high school, you are not going to get away with this . . ." A serious discussion about high school barriers and facilitators is essential prior to the transition to high school.

Implications for Teacher Educators

Teacher educators, although not working in public K-12 schools, may still use this research to help inform and transform the curricula they teach aspiring teachers. In addition to the standards new teachers have to meet and courses they have to complete, this research suggests there should be a part of the pre-service teachers' plan of study that relates to understanding the significance of the transition period. I am aware that pre-service teachers must take methods courses in order to get a teaching license. Within those classes, there should be a significant section on transition, especially for teachers who will teach eighth and ninth grades.

Secondly, teacher educators could use the information from this research study to help their students prepare and plan for obstacles they will face when they enter the classroom. With this research, teacher educators can help pre-service teachers be proactive rather than reactive to the topic of transition. Pre-service teachers could begin their transition plan or framework before they complete the teacher education program.

In addition to the transition piece, teacher educators should also consider and share with the pre-service teachers that, while the transition to high school is difficult for most students, African American males in particular have another layer to stack on top of the transition difficulties. Pre-service teachers need to understand or, at the very least, be aware of the complexities of the African American male in American schools.

One recommendation for teacher educators is program evaluation. Teacher education programs provide multicultural education courses, cultural foundations courses, etc. These courses should be examined for effectiveness and efficiency to measure the impact of the courses on the teachers and their practice.

Not only does this research have implications for teacher educators, there are also implications for district and site-based administrators.

Implications for School Administrators

At the district level, there are numerous program managers and academic coaches. There are two English/language arts program managers, one for K-5 and the other for 6-12; there are two social studies, science, and math program managers as well who serve the same grade spans. In conjunction with the program managers, the academic coaches go out to the schools and demonstrate or model how particular skills should look in the classroom. The district leaders should use this same concept and apply it to middle school to high school transition. A transition program manager and transition coaches should be hired for the district. The transition program manager and transition coaches would go out to middle and high schools and facilitate how to create a transition plan or framework for students, specifically African American males.

In addition to sending personnel to each site, the district leaders should make transition professional development offerings available for teachers and principals to attend. Information similar to that which is presented in this study should be shared with them. The words of the students need to be revealed to these professionals so they will take this notion of transition seriously. I want them to know, from this study especially, that, if they would listen, the students would tell them exactly how they can help and support them during the transition period.

If the district personnel take on the responsibility of designating funds for transition planning and professional development, there must be an evaluation tool or some way to hold all who are involved accountable. The accountability portion would be for all high schools to develop a transition plan. In this plan, teachers and principals would have to indicate the facilitators they are employing to assist their students in a successful transition to high school.

Implications for Classroom Teachers

The classroom teacher is critical. The implications for classroom teachers are dire. First and most importantly, the classroom teachers must establish relationships with their students. The participants in this study stated more than once that they wanted their teachers to know more about them. Classroom teachers need to understand their students. They need to recognize their developmental stage and what is happening with their students in relation to identity construction (gender, race, and ethnicity) and the changes that are occurring in the daily lives of their students.

Secondly, classroom practitioners need to be aware of the skills and tools their students do or do not possess. In this study, the participants were very clear when they stated they came to high school lacking some of the skills they needed to be academically successful. It is the classroom teacher's responsibility to ascertain his or her students' capabilities and limitations and create facilitators to support them and help them be successful.

Next, classroom teachers need to realize that their expectations of their students do make a difference. The participants in this study stated that knowing what their teachers expected of them helped them to transition successfully. Teachers need to continue to have high expectations for their students and continue to articulate those expectations to them. As a part of expectations, classroom teachers need to be particularly careful of making stereotypical judgments about students, specifically African American male students, in their classrooms. Teachers need to take extra care and analyze themselves and the manner in which they view students.

Implications for Future Research

Based on the analysis and the results/findings in this study, below are the implications for further research.

Using a larger sample size for both the quantitative portion and the qualitative segment of the study in several different sites within the school district would give a better rate of generalizability and the results/findings may be more comprehensive and represent many students rather than a few.

If a researcher could locate a site or group of sites where a high school transition framework or plan is operating successfully, studies can be done to examine the components of the plan and check to see if the framework encompasses any of the facilitators mentioned by the participants in this study.

I would still like to see more investigation into the personal aspect of transitioning from middle school to high school for African American males.

What are some of the other personal barriers and facilitators not mentioned by the participants in this study?

I would like for a similar study to be done with ninth-grade African American girls to examine the barriers and facilitators they feel are significant during the transition to high school and compare the differences and similarities of the African American girls and boys.

I would like for a similar study to be done with ninth-grade Hispanic males to examine the barriers and facilitators they feel are significant during the transition to high school and compare the differences and similarities of the Hispanic males and the African American males.

I would like for a similar study to be done with ninth-grade African American males from different socioeconomic backgrounds and examine the barriers and facilitators they feel are significant during the transition to high school and compare the differences and similarities between and among the various socioeconomic backgrounds.

Bibliography

Alspaugh, J. (1998). Achievement loss associated with transition to middle school and high school. *The Journal of Educational Research, 92,* 20-26.

Bailey, D. F., & Paisley, P. O. (2004). Developing and nurturing excellence in African American male adolescents. *Journal of Counseling & Development, 82,* 1.

Benner, A., & Graham, S. (2009). The transition to high school as a developmental process among multiethnic urban youth. *Child Development, 80,* 356-376.

Capstick, C. D. (2008). The ninth grade transition: Reinventing the start of high school. *Dissertation Abstracts International Section A: Humanities and Social Sciences, 68,* 3293.

Cauley, K., & Jovanovich, D. (2006). Developing an effective transition program for students entering middle school. *Clearing House, 80,* 15-25.

Chapman, M., & Sawyer, J. (2001). Bridging the gap for students at risk of school failure: A social work-initiated middle to high school transition program. *Children & Schools, 23,* 235-236.

Chmelynski, C. (2003). *Ninth grade academies help students adjust to high school.* National School Board Association.

Creswell, J. W. (2005). Educational research: Planning, conducting, and evaluating quantitative and qualitative research. New Jersey: Pearson.

Creswell, J. W. (2003). Research design: Qualitative, quantitative, and mixed methods approaches. California: Sage Publications.

Cushman, K. (2006). Help us make the 9th grade transition. *Educational Leadership, 63,* 47-52.

Eccles, J. S., Lord, S, & Midgley, C. (1991). What are we doing to early adolescents? The impact of educational contexts on early adolescents. *American Journal of Education,* 521-542.

Forgan, J. W., & Vaughn, S. (2000). Adolescents with and without LD make the transition to middle school. *Journal of Learning Disabilities, 33,* 33.

Gall, M., Borg, W., & Gall, J. (1996). *Educational research: An introduction.* New York: Longman Publishers.

Garson, G. D. (2002). *Guide to writing papers, theses, and dissertations.* New York: Marcel Dekker, Inc.

Gause, C. P. (2008). Integration matters. New York: Peter Lang Publishing, Inc.

Graham, S., Taylor, A., & Hudley, C. (1998). Exploring achievement values among ethnic minority early adolescents. *Journal of Educational Psychology, 90,* 606-620.

Heck, R., & Mahoe, R. (2006). Student transition to high school and persistence: Highlighting the influences of social divisions and school contingencies. *American Journal of Education, 112,* 418-446.

Heller, R., Calderon, S., & Medrich, E. (2003). Academic achievement in the middle grades: What does research tell us? *Southern Education Board.*

Hymel, S., Comfort, C., Schoner-Reichl, K., & McDougall, P. (1996). Academic failure and school dropout: The influence of peers. *Social Motivation,* 313-345.

Isakson, K., & Jarvis, P. (1999). The adjustment of adolescents during the transition into high school: A short term longitudinal study. *Journal of Youth and Adolescence,* 28.

Ladson-Billings, G., & Tate, W. (1995). Toward a critical race theory of education. *Teachers College Record, 97,* 47-68.

Letrello, T., & Miles, D. (2003). The transition from middle school to high school: Students with and without learning disabilities share their perceptions. *The Clearing House, 76,* 212-215.

Lindsay, D. (1997). Transition from middle school to high school: Worthington Kilbourne High School model. *American Secondary Education, 26,* 21-26.

McIntosh, J., & White, S. (2006). Building for freshman success: High schools working as professional learning communities. *American Secondary Education, 34,* 40-49.

Mizelle, N. B. (2005). Moving out the middle school. *Educational Leadership, 62,* 56-60.

Morgan, P. L., & Hertzog, C. J. (2001). Designing comprehensive transitions. *Principal Leadership, 7,* 10-18.

Pluviose, D. (2008). Remedying the black male "crisis." *Diverse Issues in Higher Education, 25,* 5.

Potter, L., Schlisky, S., Stevenson, D., & Drawdy, D. (2001). The transition years: When it's time to change. *Principal Leadership, 1,* 10-18.

Sleeter, C., & Delgado Bernal, D. (2003). Critical pedagogy, critical race theory, and antiracist education: implications for multicultural education. *Handbook on Multicultural Research.* San Francisco: Jossey-Bass.

Smith, J. E. (1997). Effects on eighth-grade transition programs on high school retention and experiences. *The Journal of Educational Research, 90,* 144.

Somers, C., Owens, D., & Piliawsky. M. (2009). A study of high school dropout prevention and at-risk ninth graders' role models and motivations for school completion. *Education, 130,* 2.

Wyatt, S. (2009). The brotherhood: Empowering adolescent African-American males toward excellence. *Professional School Counseling, 12,* 6.

African American Men and Boys: Powerful Writers

Pamela Fitzpatrick
University of North Carolina, Greensboro
Orange County Schools, Educator

Abstract

In this paper, I will explore the best ways to help our middle school and high school young men find their unique and resplendent voices in writing. We are losing our young men. Too many drop out of school, and I believe the way we teach writing may be part of the problem. Writing should be as enjoyable as talking, and it is not for so many of our young men. Rather, it is a laborious chore characterized by protracted, ineffectual grammar lessons. Based on my experience as a teacher and my educational research project, I will explore how the judicious use of film clips and simple scaffolding techniques can be used to help our boys and young men voices flower.

"Mrs. Fitzpatrick, I do not like to write; it's boring," divulged Marcus.

"Well, you have a story within you. What do you like to write or read about in your free time?" I whispered.

Marcus responded, "Nothing'."

"Marcus, think again. I always see you working on song lyrics. Your rapping is so artistic. You also read a hip-hop magazine. Both writing lyrics and reading nonfiction is important writing and reading."

"It is?" he replied in a puzzled tone.

Conversations like this can be heard in classrooms all over the county. Students, particularly males, claim they are not partial to writing, but I believe they are. I maintain that, if young men were encouraged to find their voices in writing, if they realized that educators recognized their life experiences as valuable, they would write more and better. It is the responsibility of educators to forge a path towards the development of a celebration of the resplendence of voice in our young men. Moreover, having experienced helping young men discover voice, I can say that teachers who give this help will experience the pure joy of authentic, affirming teaching.

In this paper, I will explore how educators may best help young men write with greater expression and personal agency. The pedagogical practices I will suggest are based on educational research I did through Elon University's ETLP (Elon Teaching and Learning Partnership) during the 2008-2009 school year. This qualitative study, funded by the Arthur Vining Davis Foundation, examined the types of writing prompts and writing introductory lessons that would most resonate with boys to produce good writing. Additionally, I examined pre-writing and post-writing surveys of the boys and made overall observations of the behavior of the male students during different kinds of lessons. Further, I will add some of my observations that I have made about boys and writing in my career as a teacher. I began teaching in 1976. Note that all descriptions of students and teachers are composites of people I have worked with as an educator. No description describes a specific person.

Problems for Young Men, Salient Concerns for Teachers

All of us have heard the disheartening statistics about young men dropping out of school, particularly young men of color. Jay P. Green and Marcus Winters of The Manhattan Institute of Policy Research reported in *Leaving Boys Behind: Public High School*

Graduation Rates (2009) that, in 2003, the high school graduation rate was 48% for African American males. What happened to the other 52%? Why were they not with their peers? Is the way writing is taught contributing to the drop out crisis? I think it is, and I assert that we need a boy-friendly approach to teach purposeful, practical, and joyful writing that may actually help girls, too. As we see our young men flower within the multiple parameters of quality writing, we can, hopefully, forge a closer connection between each young man and his indispensable voice in writing, thereby keeping him in school. I want boys to understand that voice is powerful; it is for him to hone and then share with others. Unfortunately, too many of our young men do not believe others think their thoughts are valuable, particularly teachers. I would like to change that perception; I would also like to encourage teachers, particularly females, to ask themselves if they clearly articulate to boys, in word and *action*, that male voices have consequence.

Are our lessons high-interest, interactive, and relevant to the boys' lives now, today? Or are they repetitively presented as isolated writing skills that can be used for sentences today and on some future day when grammar will be tested? If writing is a soulless, formulaic, almost mathematical procedure that is ruled by protracted, mind-numbing grammar lessons that add nothing to authentic writing, why should our young men look at writing as an expressive art? Regrettably, that is how far too many boys (and girls for that matter) are taught to write. Writing should be as pleasurable as talking, and it just is not for many of our young men. Why do so many of our young men consider writing such a gruesome chore, and what can educators do about it?

What Educators Can Do

I think I can anticipate what some of you are thinking. You are thinking that, in your state, you have state writing assessments in 4th, 7th, and 10th grades, for example. What about those usually dry assessments?, you may ask. The students typically have to write to a five-paragraph formula, and all of us want our students to do well on these tests, so what should be done?

Well, admittedly there are many types of state-mandated writing assignments that are not connected to song lyrics, gaming, hunting, sports, family, or art and would not be considered elevating experiences. True, but what has been the upshot of forcing a formulaic program of writing on our young men? Have they flowered in their ability to write? Do they love writing and look forward to the opportunity? For the most part, no, they do not. Therefore, another approach is needed that respects and recognizes the life histories, knowledge, and interests of our students. After we draw them into the glories and pleasures of writing, then we can teach them to take a prescribed state writing assessment. The way I think of this is, "First one thing, then another."

Let me tell you a story. Years back, I was asked by an 8th grade English teacher to test a recalcitrant student, D. (not his real name) in reading and writing. She wanted to know what his reading level was because he was not doing any work in class—nothing. She was massively frustrated with him because he wanted to establish a tacit agreement with her, which was, "If you leave me alone, I will not disrupt class." This experienced, caring, and tenacious teacher, Mrs. M. (not her real name) was not willing to give up. I tested D. using an informal reading inventory, and he tested at the 9th grade instructional reading level. I came to his class a few more times to talk with him, and we discussed his interests outside of school. D. divulged, "I'm with my father and brother. We do a lot of hunting; now it is turkey hunting season." In fact, most of the meat the family ate was killed and slaughtered by the family, for the family. As he spoke about hunting, his demeanor changed; he looked at me intently, and he spoke eloquently and confidently. He could teach me about something in which he had an expertise, if you will. He spoke of different hunting techniques and the variety of methods he used to hunt certain animals. D. spoke with such passion, interest and enjoyment about the time he spent with his father and brother as they hunted. "My mom used the meat that we hunt for our meals. We have a freezer full of dinners."

Slaughtering meat was also in D.'s repertoire of skills, and he patiently explained how he labored to dismantle a carcass. Frequently, as he explained hunting to me, I had to stop him to elaborate on the meanings of some of the words he was using like "blind" and "camo." D. has real knowledge about living off the land. Why is this not recognized by some teachers as worthwhile? His knowledge is real knowledge. D.'s cultural capital is the cultural capital of the rural South where hunting is a beloved and respected part of the cohesiveness of family. When I asked him to write about his experiences—experiences that were an integral part of his character and family—he wrote beautifully; he had voice.

When I told his teacher that D. was trying to hoodwink her by not reading and writing, she was pleased and eager to try a different tack. Since she knew she could appropriately push him because his reading skills were on level, she used her fair but firm methods to demand better and more age-appropriate reading and additional writing pieces of quality.

The same teacher also discussed with me that formal writing, to a prompt, is a requirement in every English class and many other classes. Therefore, many students acquiesce to teacher demands and write formulaically and without passion; some write reluctantly and without interest; and a handful refuse to write at all. Therefore, I will explore the types of writing prompts students enjoyed—and responded to—and the types of prompts and scaffolding that produced quality student writing.

I will also delve into how and why students respond to writing prompts and the "what" behind student writing. What do students want to write about? What interests them? Why do too many children not develop their unique, flowering voices? What can teachers do to help? Are there any simple techniques teachers can use to help student start to flourish as writers? If so, what are these uncomplicated pedagogical practices?

I will look at these pedagogical practices and how they were effective, or not, with one student: K.

K. as a Writer

Perhaps an introduction to a young man, whom I will call K. (not his real name), will illuminate the types of prompts that elicit the most powerful responses. I worked with K. and I found him intriguing. K. is an extremely bright African American 14-year old male. He is considered academically able by all of his classmates and teachers, and he has some decided opinions about school. What kind of young man is K.? What are his interests? He is a tall, athletic young man who likes football, most sports, really. He also has a well-developed musical and artistic sensibility. His musical tastes range from old school, gospel, and rhythm and blues to the contemporary sounds of hip-hop. Moreover, K. is a boy who likes fun. He loves the comedy of Jaime Fox, Eddie Murphy, Martin Lawrence, Chris Rock, Jeff Foxworthy, Richard Pryor, and especially Bill Cosby. K. also likes to write, particularly when the writing prompt is appropriately introduced.

Let us see, by way of illustration, how K. responds to a typical prompt that is offered without context. In this case, K. was asked to sit and write.

This opening prompt is a four-minute quick write, and this type of prompt is typically used in schools to start a lesson. In this class, the lesson is about weather. (I am reproducing K.'s responses exactly as he wrote them without any corrections.)

What is the weather like in your state?

K.'s response: (State's name) in the summer is hot it may get to the 90's maybe even 100's. In 2007 there was even a drought, may have hurricanes. In fall it is warm at beginning then cools down to about 50s or low 60s.

In winter its cold in the 30s or 40s, we might get snow. We had snow last year twice. In the spring its nice & about 60s or 70s.

K's lifeless response is a direct reflection of the lifelessness of the question. No part of K. comes out in this response. A question that does not require the student to think will result in an answer that is devoid of serious thought. K.'s response is linear in that he begins with writing about the summer and then moves on to the fall and winter. However, he mechanically answered the question without offering himself to his writing. Lifelessness 1; voice 0.

This may have been acceptable part of getting his ideas down for a prewriting exercise if K. was writing for a standardized writing test. However, I care about a great deal more than the formulaic writing of the state assessment when I teach my students. I can assume because you are reading this article that you do, too.

K.'s poor use of conventions illustrates a lack of attentiveness to the mechanics. His prose demonstrates a deficiency not in his ability to use proper conventions but his lack of motivation to do so with this prompt. He has no interest in constructing an engaging response.

Same Day: My second question was about weather after I showed a short film clip. This was a four-minute quick write.

What did you learn about the weather? What intrigues you?
K.'s response: Weather is predictable by the things around us. You can predict anything with the study of meteorology. I learned that the troposphere is where the weather happens, and it stores the air we breathe. Also, the clouds keep us warm over night. but the weather stays the same.

Later I asked, *"Did the film help you understand weather to a greater degree?"* This was a two-minute quick write.
K.'s response: Yes, a little because I knew there were meteorologist, but I didn't know some of the cool facts.

What was the difference between K.'s first, second, and third responses? Why were the responses more reflective of K.'s voice? The only difference is that I showed a short documentary film clip about meteorology before K.'s second response. I gave no instruction about sentence structure, punctuation, vocabulary, or paragraphing.

Moreover, what was particularly striking about K.'s writing was the improved mechanics of the second and third responses. When K. finds relevance or connection to a topic, he not only writes better—he writes with more correct conventions, which made my teacher's heart skip a beat! How could this be? How could K.'s writing change so dramatically within one seventy-minute class period? My answer is simple. To prompt K. and the rest of the students to write, I showed them a short film clip featuring a young African American male meteorologist. The meteorologist spoke about his work and his interest in all modes of weather. This ten-minute film clip was straightforward and instructional; it was not created for entertainment.

Additionally, since the meteorologist was African American, he seemed to have an appeal to K.; this is a salient point. We need to include multitudinous examples of people of color involved in myriad activities and jobs to best stimulate our African American males to write. This not only shows respect for our students and their cultures, it shows what may be possible in careers.

What accounts for K.'s improved response after the film? I think it partially was film itself, which I included in my instruction using a BDA (Before, During, and After) lesson format. Before the film, I introduced the topic of meteorology; during the film, I asked the students to watch to understand the work the meteorologist did in a day, and afterwards the students wrote about and discussed the film. (It is worth noting that watching any film without talking, writing, and discussion is not a sound pedagogical practice.) Film is a medium that offers instantaneous accessibility to K. and all of my middle school students. When a short film is popped in, they open their eyes and watch. I have often experienced the phenomenal impact of film over the last thirty years, and I have seen the interest the visual imagery of film can provoke.

After watching for ten minutes, K. was able to extract meaning from the film—which, of course, is text—and express himself clearly and succinctly in writing He was not alone. The rest of the class watched the film clip assiduously; they sat up; their eyes opened wide, and they gazed forthwith. Could including film clips in writing prompts help our students write with a more empowered voice? It could. Could we as teachers help more students find their voice by thoughtfully using film clips? We could. Did using culturally sensitive film clips help K.? I think so.

I will let K.'s voice close this piece. (K. did not have a chance to proofread this writing.)

> *What did I learn about the weather? I learned things I didn't know. I didn't know how the hurricane people found about hurricanes and that was how they looked when they were working. I also didn't know what the meteorologist did behind the scenes, and everything he had to do. So I learned a lot from the film.*

Is this the level of writing we want for K.? No. Could he do better? Yes, he could. We want his writing to become richer and more well developed, and I know teachers would like a student like K. to find his unique voice. The techniques I suggested in this article are but a first series of steps to help our young men flower as writers as they develop respect, and achieve respect, for their resplendent voices.

Please note that all descriptions of students and teachers are composites of people I have worked with as an educator. No description describes a specific person.

Bibliography

Green, J. & Winters, M. Manhattan Institute of Policy Research. (2009, April). Leaving boys behind: Public high school graduation rates.
Retrieved November 26, 2010, from http://www.manhattan-institute.org/html/cr_48.htm

Biography

Pamela Fitzpatrick is a third-year Ph.D. student at the University of North Carolina at Greensboro in Educational Studies: Cultural Foundations and has worked as an educator in Orange County Schools since 1996. Pamela is a National Board Certified Teacher in English/language arts and is the 2009-2010 North Carolina Middle School Association Teacher of the Year for district 5, which includes 15 counties from Orange County to Guilford County.

She has presented papers at numerous East Coast conferences. Her two current areas of scholarship are African American boys and writing and the 20th century German philosopher and feminist, Edith Stein. During 2008-2009, Pamela was an Elon teacher scholar through the Elon Teaching and Learning Partnership, and this is where she started her educational research on boys and writing.

Contact Information:

Ms. Pamela Fitzpatrick
Dept: ELC/SOE
University of North Carolina, Greensboro
Greensboro, NC 27402

Black Male Masculinity in Cinema: De-sexed, Feminized, and Absent

Pearlie Strother-Adams
Western Illinois University

Introduction

Guerrero (1995) argues the black male image in commercial cinema is a paradoxical mix of stereotype and adoration driven by a "defined yet complexly contradictory formula" (395). As comedian, writer Paul Mooney reminds, the black man is the most imitated of all around the world. Mooney teases, "Everybody wants to be black, but nobody wants to be a black." Thus, black male masculinity as traditionally depicted in mainstream Hollywood cinema represents an archetypal type that has evolved overtime from a cast of controversial and colorful characters, both fictional and factual, to become the composite stereotypical criminal, the thug, the gangsta, the drug dealer, the addict (Campbell, 1995). However, the archetypal tom (Uncle Tom) has also reemerged as a relevant representation of black male masculinity in modern film. Further, since the creation of D.W. Griffith's *Birth of a Nation* (1915), Hollywood has wrestled with the archetypal "buck," sexually on the prowl, a rapist, the savage (Campbell, 1995; Lule, 2001), his black body glistening on the big screen, as he is often shown shirtless with upper body muscles rippling and intricately well defined, a classic "six-pack," the sports figure described in Rich Majors' *Cool Pose* (1993). He is a young Muhammad Ali, good looking, smooth, "dance like a butterfly, sting like a bee," physically powerful, a Michael "Air" Jordan, soaring, flying, strong, god-like, a machine, but sometimes funny and disarming, like Eddie Murphy and Will Smith and, more recently in hip hop culture, a Fifty Cent or a Kanye West, both hardcore, uncombed, raw, sexy, uncontained, bound in gold and silver chains, "bling-bling!"

70

On the other hand, such images, popular media symbols of black male masculinity, are collectively taboo and are forever indelibly imprinted in the mainstream white society's psyche as a "menace to society," a threat to what are considered traditional white ideals, white standards and particularly white male sensibilities about intimate relations between white females and black males. According to Gates (2004), black male masculinity is regarded as a threat to white mainstream culture because of its being attracted to and attractive to white women (5).

Yet Hollywood insists on pairing black and white characters and the new trend in the cinematic genre known as the buddy film, which will be discussed in this work, is the pairing of the black male as the lead, the hero, and a young, popular, white female star as his buddy. Guerrero (1993) offers there is a reluctance in mainstream cinema to place a black star in a film without a white co-star or a white context because of the presumed need to offer a point of identification for white audiences (239). Consequently, neither the black community, black issues/problems, particularly involving race, nor the black female exist in these films.

While scholars have explored, to some degree in the literature, the problems involving the absence of the black community and race in these films (Guerrero, 1993; Aims, 1996; Gates, 2004), it is important that it is noted here that little has been said about the absence of black females, who remain a strong and necessary component in the black community and are major contributors to the survival of the black male as he is forced to continue screaming over and over again metaphorically to America sentiments expressed by the late blues singer Muddy Waters in his signature song, "I'm a man!"

Thus, this work is two-fold. First, it explores cinematic representation of black male masculinity in the buddy film, which features leading black male actors as heroes paired with white female buddies and maintains that this standard, Hollywood representation of black male masculinity functions to uphold traditional white hegemonic beliefs, values and practices particularly in regard to white society's notions about interracial relations between the black male and the white female. Second, this work looks at the replacement of realistic black male masculinity, which includes love, intimate relations or sexuality, community, roots, politics and other human factors, with an unrealistic puppet controlled image of a man that functions for the purpose of putting at ease and pleasing white society and, even though interracial relations remain unacceptable, the message in cinema is clear—the white female represents the "norm" in terms of true womanhood, and the assumption in Hollywood is that no other representation is wanted or required.

Hence, the works that are analyzed in this paper are traditional buddy films. They are as follows: Denzel Washington in *Pelican Brief* (1993) and *Bone Collector* (1999); Will Smith and Martin Lawrence in *Bad Boys* (1995); Morgan Freeman in *Kiss the Girls* (1997) and *Along Came a Spider* (2001). I will also use one action drama, that I have labeled simply "Uncle buddy/Best buddy." Here some definition is required. In these films, the lead black male as hero becomes so closely connected to a child buddy, often a female, as to take on the role of a father or even, ironically, a mother-like figure, a care giver, a throwback to the archetypal "Uncle Tom" from Harriet Beecher Stowe's *Uncle Tom's Cabin* (1852) and, from a cinematic perspective, the relationship between Bill Bojangles Robinson and Shirley Temple (1930s). Similarly, there is resemblance to the archetypal Mammy, a character who builds her whole life, it seems, around the white family she cares for, especially the children. Such is the case in the modern drama that is explored here, *Missing in America(2005)*, featuring Danny Glover. Often in such films, an adult white female is involved and thus, true to form (the buddy film) and cinematic tradition, an unrequited love ensues. Hence, as is the case in the buddy film, there are glimpses of possible passion but such is never allowed to materialize.

Thus, it is important to explore issues around the representation of black male masculinity because such representations are highly symbolic and suggestive in nature and could prove life altering for the black community. Containment of the black male's masculinity, his sexuality, strength, ability to survive, and physical prowess, all key elements that characterize traditional male masculinity, renders the black male symbolically weak and void of manhood, effeminate, "de-sexed," but safe, non-threatening and compromised for mainstream white America. The title of Christopher Ames's groundbreaking work "Restoring the Black Man's Lethal Weapon" (1992) serves as an adequate metaphor here, for the black man's sexuality, his masculinity, his attachment and identity to his race, his politics are indeed his lethal weapon and, in the buddy film, all are in need of restoration. Second, the black male's estrangement and isolation from the black community and particularly from the black female perpetuate first the notion of the black community as the "other," an alien entity outside of the mainstream, not the norm, unimportant, powerless; while at the same time, the black male hero is also an alien loner, rootless, with no family and no home, abandoned, a spirit in the wind, a character from nowhere, a refugee who lacks normal needs, such as love and human connection to a family. Further, the total absence of the black female as a viable, seemingly logical and suitable buddy or mate sends a powerfully painful and psychologically disturbing message to America and particularly to both black women and men—that Hollywood's idea of the acceptable black male is one that comes free of the weight of the black female and a black family. Hopefully, this work contributes to this body of literature on black male masculinity and seeks to answer the following research questions:

RQ-1. Does Hollywood deliberately seek to portray black males as effeminate, de-sexed, restrained to appease mainstream white audiences?

RQ-2. Is the placement of black male heroes outside of the black community, out of reach of all that is black, even the black female and the black family, symbolic of traditional racist practices and does it communicate a low self-worth of the black female?

The black male as buddy to a white hero dates back much further than cinema in the literature. Leslie Fiedler (1966) offers the representation of the black male as the archetypal dark-skinned noble savage as buddy to the white male, a refugee from civilization, dated back to American classics such as *Huckleberry Finn* and *Moby Dick*

(15). Native Americans have also functioned in this role. In television and film, *The Lone Ranger* with his dark "Indian" sidekick Tonto serves as a symbolic classic. However, Christopher Ames (1992) informs the archetypal relationship that once existed between the stereotypical savage (black) man and the civilized man (white) has seen a reversal. The black hero is now domesticated, and paired with a white savage, as is the case in the buddy film series *Lethal Weapon*, starring Mel Gibson and Danny Glover. Thus, Ames argues the modern black male hero has lost touch with his "savage" masculinity (53). This archetype, manifested most prominently today in buddy films, takes on a new twist as Gates (2004) notes leading black male actors are now often cast as heroes with white females, instead of white males co-starring as their buddies. Gates further offers the black hero is now smart, genius, as is the case with Morgan Freeman as Alex Cross in *Kiss the Girls* and *Along Came a Spider;* Denzel Washington as Graham Gray in *Pelican Brief* and as Lincoln Rhyme in *The Bone Collector (8-12).* Their white female buddies, on the other hand, are strong, young, and physically capable. She has brawn. She is savage, capable of existing in the wilderness, like Ashley Judd as Kate in *Kiss the Girls*. She can survive in the metaphorical urban jungle. She's a kick boxer who, in the end, gets away from her attacker and helps to save other women that have been taken by him. The same is true of Angelina Jolie as Amelia in *The Bone Collector*. She is a tough cop who saves her buddy, Rhyme (Washington) in the end. The black male hero, on the other hand, is emasculated (Gates 2004, 8-12), contained and restrained. Thus, Guerrero (Black, 239) maintains such positioning of the black hero with the white buddy places the black male's body in protective custody of the white sidekick.

Further, Gates (2004) argues mainstream cinema features blacks on screen without addressing race or ethnic issues or placing them in situations where race is a factor, that is, outside of the black community, without a black context.

Background: From Sidekick to Hero

The modern detective buddy film was made popular beginning with the star power of comedian/actor Eddie Murphy in *Beverly Hills Cop* (1984, 1987, 1984); and later Danny Glover in *Lethal Weapon* (1987, 1989, 1992, 1998). In both film series, black actors Murphy and Glover, respectively, were sidekicks to a white male buddy. In the case of Murphy, his fame quickly led to a shift in role positioning and he became the lead buddy in subsequent films in the series. Murphy's star power, ability to draw large audiences to the theater, proved beneficial for up and coming black male actors. Consequently, other black actors were placed in leading roles: Denzel Washington in *Pelican Brief* (1993), *Devil in a Blue Dress* (1995), and *The Bone Collector* (1999); Will Smith and Martin Lawrence in *Bad Boys* (1995); and Morgan Freeman in *Kiss the Girls* (1997), and *Along Came a Spider* (2001). Similarly, one action drama of note that shares pivotal characteristics with the buddy film is Danny Glover's *Missing in America* (2005).

The year 2001 netted an Oscar each for best actor and best actress, respectively, for Denzel Washington (*Training Day*) and Hallie Berry (*Monster's Ball*), while veteran actor, trailblazer Sidney Poitier was honored with a lifetime achievement award. Washington, along with other black male actors, Morgan Freeman, Samuel Jackson, Will Smith, and Danny Glover, now ranks among America's most prolific, most popular and highest paid actors. However, the road to fame has not been as well paved for black female actors. One would think that, if black male actors gained such tremendous success, black female actors would rise to the top with them. In Hallie Berry's acceptance speech at the Oscars, she thanked the black female actors who had come before while acknowledging her fellow black female contemporaries. Logically, as the black male came into his own as a lead character, a hero in the buddy film, it would seem, if a female were to serve as his sidekick, it would be the black female, particularly given society's long history of interracial sexual taboos. On the contrary, it is the white female who has benefited, riding the black male's coattail, and taking on the role as his buddy, his partner, his sidekick and fantasy lover. Even more strange and unbelievable is that the black hero is taken totally out of the black community, away from all that is black, and placed in a totally white society where he is regarded as a mega genius, a brain, so special and pampered that all revolves around him. Consequently, it is up to him to come up with all of the answers and thus save white society. His life takes on new meaning as he becomes the protector and the "protected" and the defender of white society and its ideals. His context is totally race-free as if he is miraculously washed clean of the whole thing (race and politics) and, therefore, shares no part of the problems of black society, the black community, the black family, for he is totally accepted in and is a token part of this Hollywood-fabricated race-free world.

More Background: The Black Savage Remains an Issue

However, the protection of the white female from the "sexual savage" black male has remained an issue and an objective in cinema since Griffith's *Birth of a Nation,* in which black men were portrayed with threatening, out of control masculinity. It was activist journalist Ida B. Wells who warned after conducting investigations into the widespread lynching of black men that consensual relationships existed between black men and white women in many cases where black men were accused of rape and subsequently lynched mob style without a trial. Interestingly, romantic involvement between blacks and whites remains taboo in American culture and as such continues to be played out most vividly in contemporary cinema and is demonstrated best in buddy films. For, though intimacy is denied, there is talk of sex and sex play in a kind of game of untouchable cat and mouse, a play on sexually provocative words and body language. This is the case in five of the six films that were studied for this work. It would appear that, though relationships between the black male and white female are unacceptable, there is a certain appeal to the flirtation. bell hooks offers in her work *Black Looks* (1992) that this obsession is the dominant culture's way of "eating the other" or getting a little taste of the forbidden. In essence, there is an attraction.

Methods

In this work, qualitative semiotic textual analysis is used to analyze film text. Using semiotics, we can conduct analysis of film text on several levels of signification. Barthes (1957/1972) analyzed images and words on several tiers, among them are denotation, connotation and myth. Denotative meaning is literal, what we see and hear, whereas connotation is much deeper and signification takes on ideological meaning. Myth, then, says Barthes, exists in the culture and is transferred through language in the form of stereotypes and metaphors that have been naturalized in the culture. Simply put, we see them as the norm and see no other way (Barthes, 1972). Thus, semiotic analysis is the study of and interrogation of signs and symbols within text (Barthes, 1968). Careful interrogation of the representation, images of these films prove revealing in terms of Hollywood's portrayal of black male masculinity.

Theoretical Framework

Critical cultural scholars offer a litany of research on culture and race. Critical cultural theory involves the interrogation of a data set (film text, such as character, plot, setting and theme) with an interest in identifying its ideological bias and the implications of this bias for power relations. Thus, critical cultural scholars believe that ideology and power characterize the social experience. According to Baxter and Babbie (2003), the goal of the critical cultural scholar is to both enlighten and emancipate members of a society or group by showing whose interests are served and what are the underlying values of a communicative practice (63), such as the representation of the black male hero in the buddy film as alien-other, passive, feminized and de-sexed.

Though the appearance of black males in such high profile roles would seem to be an accomplishment, as Manthia Diawara argues, such images of racial "otherness" in cinema tend to be merely tokenism and not representative of the specificity of black experience (12). Further, to feminize the black male is an attempt to show him as less than a man, as weak.

Guerrero (1993) argues the message is that black subordination to the system is required to solve the problems of the dominant white culture (242). Indeed, as is evident in the buddy film, the black male is not accorded the same liberties as the white male hero, as cinema reflects the cultural ideology of mainstream society. Thus, the black male hero plays second fiddle to his white female buddy. In short, Hollywood maintains the traditions deeply rooted in the American hegemony. Simply put, the rule remains intact. In American media, including cinema, "Art imitates life." Thus, the black male hero stands in the shadow of the white female and, in many respects, is merely a token and really no hero at all in the eyes and minds of many white viewers, at least not in the traditional sense, for it is the white female who takes on this role. She is the fortress upon which he has to lean.

Diawara explains whites occupy the center of the narrative space and blacks occupy the periphery constructed only in relation to the white—protagonists (12). Space is related to power, and those at the center—whites—have power and those on the periphery— "other"—do not. Thus, the black hero is not allowed to occupy the traditional space of power—the center, the place designated for the traditional white male hero. To gain acceptance, Hollywood places the white woman at the center in that she is allowed all the qualities of the true American cinematic hero. Hence, it is a way of containing black male masculinity so no threat is posed that offends the white audience.

Analysis

Containment: Passive, Effeminate and De-sexed

Guerrero (1993) maintains the biracial buddy film does not offer a positive representation of black masculinity but instead places the black body in the "protective custody" of the white lead or co-star and, therefore, in conformity with mainstream white sensibilities and expectations of what blacks should be (239).

If we look back as far as the 1800s, we note that mainstream media have promoted the idea of the white female as the standard and the object of the American male's desire whether such presumed desire was welcomed or uninvited, as was the case with black men. In *Birth of a Nation,* the white female is held out as the object of the black man's desire, an image used to stereotype black males as "beast rapists," a term made popular by Southern white newspaper editors (Raper, 1969). The buddy film continues this tradition, though more subtle, less obvious—the black male is no longer the savage rapist. He is passive, yet desirous of his white female buddy.

The message remains the same—the white female is still the one to have, even as she continues to be off-limits, taboo, unobtainable as we see in *Pelican Brief* with Gray Grantham (Denzel Washington), a *Washington Post* reporter who investigates the story of a brief written by law student Darby Shaw (Julia Roberts) that implicates the president and White House officials in the murder of two senators. The two, Gray and Darby, both young, intelligent and attractive, join forces, working closely together. In the original John Grisham novel, sexual attraction between Gray and Darby is evident and, at the novel's end, Gray, who is white, joins Darby at her hideaway. However, the irony in all of this is that, though the white female is off-limits in cinema, she is presented as not only the acceptable standard beauty in white hegemonic society, but also the best choice for the black male, for all males and, thus, is depicted in these films as being overwhelmingly desirable to the black man, even though untouchable and not obtainable, for mainstream cinema continues to portray her as off-limits and taboo for the black man who, in the buddy film, takes on the role of protector of her honor. At the film's end she boards a plane that will take her away to a remote island. He looks on, doting, like a dejected lover. She runs back to him only to kiss him on his cheek. At the film's end, Darby sits on a far-away Caribbean island as Gray is interviewed, and the question arises as to whether Darby existed at all. The idea of her as a fantasy plays into the minds of viewers who may have a problem with even the fact that a relationship might have been a thought. It is suggested that she was instead a composite of sources, a figment of Gray's imagination and, in the end, he admits "too good to be true." Gates (2004) offers: "at least too good for him" (11). Throughout the film, there is obvious camera play that zeroes in on innocent touching by the two, a play with a kind of lustful magnetism. Two examples are when Gray and Darby sit in the car together looking over some evidence, and his long black fingers touch her contrasting white inner arms gently. In another scene, Darby lies in bed, her white skin glowing in the dark, and Gray sits along the side of the bed, his dark black skin glistening. The camera zooms in for a close-up as Gray looks lovingly, dotingly at Darby, who is exhausted and barely awake. It is obvious that Hollywood makes a deliberate attempt to suggest to the audience that they did not see what they think they saw, thus further playing into the idea of Darby as a fantasy, all in Gray's passively lustful head. It is an obvious denial of the possibility of a relationship between the two. In the end, Darby is safe in her hideaway, not only from her enemies but, more important for movie sales, safe from viewers having any thought of her having a relationship with Gray. In the end, he smiles a knowing smile of love and desire for her and all the world to see via television, and she smiles back, a show of connectedness that he cannot even see. Thus, she receives his message via television: that she is much in his favor, still the object of his desires, the recipient of his most gentle, hidden, affectionate gesture and fantastical desire, even as she remains on a pedestal, unobtainable, a fantasy, consequently leaving him with nothing, no evidence of her existence for, historically, the white female is to remain taboo, untouchable to the black male. Yet, it is important that she remain the ultimate symbol of beauty, the standard of which to aspire, the object of desire, even unwelcomed desire.

Further, though it may appear to be quite a leap for some, images of the black man as being totally enamored with the white female is a throwback to *Birth of a Nation*, in which black males are depicted as lusting after white females. This in and of itself is a negative stereotype directed at black male masculinity that harkens back to the archetypal savage buck.

In *Bone Collector*, Lincoln Rhyme (Denzel Washington), a genius detective who is paralyzed from an accident while on the job, and Amelia Donaghy (Angelina Jolie) as a young beat-patrol cop work together to stop a serial killer. Amelia does the legwork while Rhymes, who is the brain—literally, as his lower extremities are not functional—unravels and analyzes the clues. Amelia is introduced as the physical force, the masculine one: "A police officer's tools of the trade lie strewn on the floor, boots, belt, gun" (Gates 16). The implication is that these belong to her male lover; however, in a role reversal, the film provides quite a jolt for the audience as they learn that Amelia is the brawny cop and that it is her male lover who complains about her lack of emotional commitment to the relationship, likening the night to another "slam-bam-thank-you-ma'm," a sentiment generally directed at callous men. As Gates (2004) argues, Amelia is masculinized, whereas Rhymes is "feminized" (17). Rhymes is depressed and planning his "final transition" or suicide. He is bedridden and physically helpless. In Rhyme's physical battle with the killer, who turns out to be Richard Thompson (Orser Leland), the technician who services his heart monitor, Rhyme's one mobile extremity, his finger, is broken. It is Amelia who comes in and saves him in the end. His estranged sister and her family are brought to his side, and it appears he is happy, all thanks to Amelia. In essence, it is she who has brought it all together for him. However, he remains contained and, as Gates offers (18), unable to perform his masculinity in the traditional ways. He cannot perform sexually, for example, even though he gets the girl. Rhymes can only fathom a relationship with Amelia. The closest he gets is having her stroke his exposed, bare, crippled fingers. The idea that he is a broken man, paralyzed, paraplegic, makes him acceptable and non-threatening. Thus, it is okay for him to get the girl. The audience can sympathize with him. It is an interesting note here, however, that Rhyme's finger, his only mobile unit, was broken in the battle with Richard. It is as if his only chance of any kind of physical response to Amelia is painfully and dramatically taken away. He had earlier referred to Amelia's stroking of his naked, black hands as a molestation. Historically, such contact between the two sexes has long been forbidden and remains offensive to many in the mainstream, taboo and, if symbolic of a molestation, certainly worthy of punishment for the black male and, in this case, the breaking of the offensive part, the finger, is an act akin to a castration. Rhymes tells Amelia it is a crime to molest the handicapped.

The plot to *Bad Boys* (19995) is very conveniently written. Julie learned of Matt through her friend, Max, who was murdered. Therefore, she only trusts Matt. When she calls the police department, Matt is out of town and Marcus is asked to pretend to be Matt because it is feared that she might flee. However, the charade is continued beyond logic, and Marcus and Matt end up exchanging roles. This is the device of containment, as Marcus is married. However, there is a game of cat and mouse with sex.

In both *Kiss the Girls* and *Along Came a Spider*, Morgan Freeman as Alex Cross is a genius, a brain, not physical, but a thinker, not dangerous, a scholar and author of several books. His female partners are Kate and Jezzie Flannigan (Monica Potter), respectively. In the film adaptations of James Patterson's two Alex Cross novels, the main character Alex is taken out of his home neighborhood of Washington, D.C. and placed in predominately all-white communities. In the novels, Alex is sometimes featured at home with his black family, dealing with crime in his own community. He lives with his grandmother and his two children. In the novel, his wife is dead. In both novels, he has a relationship with his co-star. In *Along Came a Spider*, he falls in love with Jezzie, his detective partner, and has a sexual relationship, only to be hurt by her betrayal. However, in the film, no such relationship is allowed, not even a hint. In *Kiss the Girls*, he goes on to fall in love with Kate and share one night of sexual passion with her. However, in the film, these two plan a dinner, only to have it interrupted by the killer. Their mutual attraction, however, is made obvious. It is interesting that Alex is sexualized in the novels. His body is described as being strong, sculpted. His torso is admired by Kate (Patterson, "Kiss," 290). Both women compare Alex to Muhammad Ali. Such representation, Gates (2004) says, makes him a powerful representation of black male masculinity (13). However, Freeman as Alex Cross seems to have accomplished something that Washington did not accomplish in *Pelican Brief*, even though he (Washington) is the black sex symbol. In *Kiss the Girls*, he (Freeman as Alex) does get Kate, a young, attractive, smart woman as a love interest. What is overlooked here is that Freeman is an older man and thus less threatening to the mainstream audience. He is less of a sex symbol, less the black "buck" and, therefore, less likely a threat to white males. It is interesting to note here that the villain explains to Alex (Freeman) in the end that they are really no different and that, if he, Alex, would look a little deeper, he would find that the same animalistic tendencies exist in him. He taunts Alex with this as Alex tries to convince him to give up. This is a highly symbolic scene. It speaks to the issue of the cinematic containment of all that is wild and even sexual in Alex. However, the audience is reminded that it is just beneath the surface, held at bay for the purpose of protecting the white female. Thus, as we reflect back to Washington in *Pelican Brief*, as Gray, as Gates (2004) explains there is not even a suggestion that his character, a younger man, and Roberts as Darby will get together.

Invisibility and Absence: "Missing in America"

The lead black male hero in the buddy film exists in "another world," inhabited only by whites. It is as if he is plucked out of the black community, a superhero, sent to champion the needs of and solve the problems of white society. However, the absence of and replacement of black male masculinity with effeminacy and white female masculinity, the absence of any semblance of a black community and the absence of the black woman all tell a story. In essence, cinema/Hollywood provides "meaning" through its use of or absence of certain images. Stuart Hall (1997) offers media are linked with power and the groups who "wield" power influence the dominant images. The objective of ideology, Hall maintains, is to "fix." Hall offers, when we are immersed in these images, like a fish in water, we do not question but come to accept them as the norm and are therefore less likely to interrogate them in terms of their deeper ideological meaning. Thus, it has become a norm to see white females tied to black male heroes as buddies in the buddy film. The absence of the black female is barely mentioned in previous research. Thus, the literature falls short in dealing with the dynamics of the absence of the black female as buddy, mate, lover and caregiver. Nothing is said about the fact that the white female buddy is portrayed as the object of the black heroes' desire even though she is cast as an elusive butterfly, totally unobtainable. Perhaps even more important, nothing is said about the implications for both black male and female as valuable entities in each other's lives.

Danny Glover's *Missing in America* seems an appropriate beginning here, for not only are relevant aspects of the character of the black male hero missing, but his main support and best friend, the black female, is totally missing. Richard Dyer (1988) argues mainstream cinema is predominately an articulation of white experience and that whiteness secures its dominance by seeming to be nothing in particular (44). According to Gates (2004), mainstream cinema gives little consideration to the nonwhite experience. Indeed, it would appear to be rather innocent and benign that there is a total absence of the major character's tie to any semblance to anything black. The plot is constructed so that it would appear that the main character's main purpose in life is to serve white society, even exiled white society.

In *Missing in America,* Jake (Danny Glover), a black Vietnam vet, lives secluded, in exile, deep in the forest of the Pacific Northwest with only a group of white vets as his neighbors. He has no ties to the black community. He is a caretaker who looks out for the well being of the other white vets. When Jake's long-lost friend, Henry Hocknell (David Strathairn), asks him to take care of his Eurasian daughter, Lenny Hocknell (Zoe Weizenbaum), and Jake refuses, Henry reminds him that, back in Vietnam, he (Jake) always took care of his men. A series of flashbacks are shown that feature Jake serving as the leader of his platoon back in Vietnam, serving as a patriot, fighting for his country and even sometimes sanctioning acts against those who might have been innocents to make sure that his men were not put in jeopardy. Consequently, Henry, who is dying of cancer, leaves his daughter, Lenny, with Jake. In the end, Jake connects with a white woman, Kate (Linda Hamilton), the local country storeowner. Through his conversations with Kate, we learn that he abandoned his wife because she wanted children and he did not. He learns after leaving, however, that she was pregnant and that he has a son that he has never taken the time or interest to visit. He tells Kate that he wishes his wife had not told him about the child because, as he says, you cannot miss what you never knew you had. Kate is then left to help him understand the blessing of a child. She tells him that she wished she had what he is throwing away. Such an act furthers the notion of the black man as an absentee father and an absentee husband. The title of the film, *Missing in America*, might aptly be applied as a metaphor for the state of the black man as represented in cinema, particularly in the buddy film, for he is "missing" from all that is black and a real man, ties to a community, to family, to his children, to his mate. He exists in a world outside of the norm that is Hollywood generated, a fantasy land where he has no cares or concerns about the politics and issues of the real world. In this make-believe world, Jake supplies disillusioned vets with goods from the general store and they give him firewood. Oddly, he loses Lenny, of whom he has grown to love as a daughter. She is killed accidentally by a booby trap set in the woods by Red (???), a recluse who seems to think he is still in Vietnam and that Lenny is the Vietnamese girl responsible for his life-altering facial injuries. Lenny, who is part Vietnamese, becomes an extension of Jake. Thus, she, like Jake, is a savior to the white vets. Both she and Jake are obsessed with making sure the vets are okay. When she dies, a lamb that Jake had given her as a gift emerges from the smoke of the bomb where her body lays. It is obvious that she is symbolic of a "sacrificial lamb" who, in the end, saves both Red and Jake at some level. In her innocence, she is like a Christ figure, a savior, one who forgives. She too serves to appease white society as Jake's extension. However, she is also safe. She is acceptable as a live-in child with Jake, a black man, for not only is the black man constrained in his relationship with the white female, he is also forbidden to exist in certain situations with white children, especially females. Thus, the use of a half-Vietnamese child who has a white father instead of a black father, would be more acceptable to white audiences. In the end, Jake visits the Vietnam Veterans Memorial with Kate, whom we can assume is at least a friend, for there is no intimacy. However, the hint of a relationship here is treated as if such a union would be the norm since the film has no hint of the existence of racial problems between blacks and whites.

Hence, Hall (1997) informs, "Absence signifies as much as presence." In other words, what is not shown or represented in cinema is just as important and carries just as much meaning as what is represented. While scholars make some attempts to deal with the politics of overlooking the black community in cinema (Guerrero, 1993; Ames, 1996; Gates, 2004), the absence of the black woman is not commented upon. However, through the absence of the black female from these films, Hollywood communicates that she is no longer a consideration as an adequate partner for the successful, high profile black male and that the black male of this caliber is totally out of the black female's league, whereas the white female, such as Kate in *Missing*, and other characters who will be discussed in this work, are not only present but, in a dynamic way, all-empowered heroic figures, strong, representative of the beauty standard, intuitive and skilled in their craft. In only three of the films discussed here are black women presented at all, primarily in minor roles.

In *Bone Collector*, it is interesting that the only black female in the film an attractive, strong, yet motherly nurse. Thelma (Queen Latifah) is not remotely considered as a possible love interest for the hero and she is killed off in the harshest way. Instead, it is Amelia (Angelina Jolie), the white female buddy, who is cast in this way. It is interesting to note in *Bad Boys* (1995), Matt Lowery (Will Smith) and Marcus Burnette (Martin Lawrence) are two Miami cops, "bad boys," charged with the duty of capturing murdering drug dealers and protecting a female witness to a murder, Julie Mott (Tea Leoni). Matt (Smith), as the major star and pretty rich boy, is not allowed a love interest, while Marcus (Lawrence) has a black wife and children; however, the wife is jealous and angry but she serves to contain Marcus. Guerrero (1993) offers having the black man married to a black woman can serve as a device of containment that suppresses any threat that black masculinity might seem to imply (237). Further, when black issues are presented, Guerrero (1993) explains they are presented as a problem, as is the case with Marcus's family. The real irony comes at the beginning of the film when a beautiful black actress, known as Max (Maxine Logan), who is an "escort" and an informant and old girlfriend to Matt, is shot very deliberately in the rear when she is asked to model for a white drug dealer. This is a pivotal point in the movie. One could not help wonder what the purpose was of such a demeaning display of violence perpetrated upon this beautiful black woman. The act seemed to say "You are nothing" and thus served as a metaphor for the worth of the black woman through the eyes of Hollywood. Such objectification of the black female further justifies the degrading of and violence against black women (hooks, 1992). Hence, it speaks volumes about Hollywood's perception of and representation of the worth of black women. Julie, the white actress mentioned earlier who witnesses the murder and who had also accompanied Max, survives and is placed under protective custody and thus becomes a kind of buddy to both Matt and Marcus.

In both *Kiss the Girls* and *Along Came a Spider*, the lead actor Morgan Freeman (Alex Cross) is allowed to have a sister appear briefly in both films, and a niece is among the kidnapped women in *Kiss the Girls*.

The Black Male Hero Body Under Sexual Gaze: A Reversal

Steven Neale (2000) offers cinema draws on and involves many desires. Thus, the traditional theory of spectator gaze is challenged in modern cinema. In mainstream cinema, as the past would have it, the female body was traditionally constructed, put on sexual display for male gaze. Gates therefore argues that it would appear the hero's body (the black male) should be put on display for sexual gaze since it is he who is effeminized. However, what is overlooked in such analysis is that, indeed, the black male hero's body is constructed for spectator gaze in the buddy film for the pleasure of both his side kick and the mainstream audience, many of whom regard the black male body, the body of the "other," with curiosity. In *Kiss the Girls,* for example, the hero Alex's naked, upper body is featured for sexual gaze as his female buddy Kate massages his well-defined muscles. The same is true in *Bone Collector*, even though Rhymes is paraplegic. It is his bare body that is toyed with, fondled, as he explains it, "molested" by Amelia. It is he who is said to have been "broken in two" during the accident that left him paralyzed. However, symbolically, Amelia becomes for him the physical specimen that he is not. He says that, in her, he has a fresh pair of eyes, legs and brain; thus, it is the physical cop that we see in her, his young, female, white buddy, that is the embodiment of the masculine Rhymes. He tells her that she is a lot like him and that they are both predestined. When she is faced with the gore of a difficult crime scene, he tells her that she should know that he is in there with her. He talks to her the whole time. In the end, he remarks that she has come to like the work. The transition is complete. They are one.

In *Pelican Brief*, Darby lies fully covered and half asleep in Gray's bed as he sits on side of the bed and asks her to turn and look at him. It is very obvious that Gray is the spectacle as the camera pans his bare, handsome, black face that glistens in the dark and, later in the car, Darby touches his arm gently. In the end, she kisses his cheek and walks away. The camera stays with him. He looks lost. She races back and gives him one last caress before going away to a Caribbean hideaway, while Gray is left to admit finally during a television interview that she is too good to be true, just a figment of his imagination. However, in the end, it is Gray who is positioned for spectator gaze as Darby is able to view him on the television screen. He is definitely real, handsome, with an inviting smile. Again, this plays into the idea of the hero in a reversed role, the effeminate (Gates, 14). The most revealing of such scenes takes place in *Missing in America* when Danny Glover as Jake is viewed unknowingly by his co-star Kate as he bathes in an outdoor makeshift shower. The scene is spectacular as the crisp, clear water flows over Jake's sexy, wet, black muscular body. It is very obvious that this scene is highly sexual and that Kate is much in awe of Jake's nude body and that there is sexual attraction. The camera pans up and down Jake's body very deliberately as Kate stands hidden, lusting, smiling in admiration. Later, Jake comes into Kate's store and there is a play on words. Kate starts to apologize for gazing at him as he showered, and Jake tells her that he is embarrassed, then proceeds to ask her how much it will cost him. He says he hasn't had any in a while and begins to suggest dollar figures. Just when Kate gets ready to blow up, Jake reveals that he is talking about a bottle of wine that he had taken from her store. It is obvious that this scene had to be turned into a comedy and a play of words. It would not have been acceptable any other way. In the final scene, Kate comes with Jake when he visits the Vietnam Veterans Memorial. No physical or sexual contact is allowed, although the sexual attraction is obvious. Here there is definitely a reversal of the spectacle gaze as Jake's body is presented in a way that makes him most desirable.

Conclusion

According to Stuart Hall (1997), we share an understanding of images because of "shared conceptual maps," which help us to classify the world. Such internalized concepts find their way into communication systems such as cinema through language, which Hall broadly labels discourse (speech, writing, facial expressions, gestures, clothing, settings, and matter and even space in general). This discourse comes in the form of stereotypes, myth in the form of metaphors that run through the culture (Barthes, 1972). These myths, according to Barthes (1972), pass through the culture through popular media such as cinema.

The fabrication of a fantasy world where select black males are free of themselves, of their origins, of their community and its inhabitants has serious implications for the black community as a whole. The containment of black male masculinity speaks of something more sinister than it appears. As Guerrero (1993) explains, it appears to be nothing at all; however, it reaches back a long way symbolically, all the way to slavery and Jim Crow. It denies black males access to their true selves. It takes away their manhood, an act not new to blacks in the American culture. The total absence of black women in pivotal roles in these films is crucial. Such disrespect in modern film, which represents a vision of modern society, is a gross injustice that deserves more study and comment.

Bibliography

Ames, C. (Fall, 1992). Restoring the black man's lethal weapon: Race and sexuality in contemporary cop films. *Journal of Popular Film and Television, 20*(3), 52-60.

Barthes, R. (1968). *Elements of semiology.* London: Cape.

Barthes, R. (1972). *Mythologies* (Jonathan Cape Ltd. Trans.). New York: Hill and Wang (Original work published in 1957).

Baxter, L.A. and Babbie, E. (2003). *The basics of communication research.* Boston, MA: Wadsworth.

Bird, S. E. and Dardenne, R.W. (1988). Myth chronicle and story: Exploring the narrative qualities of news. Ed. J. W. Carey *Media myths and narratives: television and the press.* Thousand Oaks, CA: Sage.

Campbell, C. P. (1995). *Race myth and news.* Thousand Oaks, CA: Sage Publications.

Diawara, M. (1993). *Black American cinema.* Ed. Manthia, Diawara. AFI Film Readers. (pp.3-26) New York: Routledge.

Dyer, R. (Autumn 1988). White. *Screen 29*(4), 44-65.

Donaldson, M. (2006). *Masculinity in the interracial buddy film.* Jefferson, NC: McFarland Company.

Fielder, L. (1982). *What was literature: Class culture and mass society.* New York: Simon & Schuster.

Gates, P. (Spring, 2004). Always a partner in crime. *Journal of Popular Film and Television, 32*(1).

Gillan, J. (2001). No one knows you're black! Six degrees of separation and the buddy film. *Cinema Journal 40,* 47-68.

Grisham, J. (1992). *The pelican brief.* New York: Doubleday.

Guerrero, E. (1993). The black image in protective custody: Hollywood's biracial buddy films of the eighties. *Black American cinema,* Ed. by Manthia Diawara,_237-246. New York: Routledge. 237-46.

Hall, S. (1997). *Representation and media.* MEF Series.

hooks, b. (1992). Black looks: Race and representative. Boston, Massachusetts: South End Press.

hooks, b. (1996). Reel to real: Race, sex, and class at the movies. New York: Routledge.

Kaplan, E. A. (1997). *Looking for the other: Feminism, film and the imperial gaze.* New York: Routledge.

Lule, J. (1995). The rape of Mike Tyson: Race, the press and symbolic types. *Critical Studies in Mass Communication 12,* 176-195.

Majors, R. and Mancini Billson, J. (1993). *Cool Pose: The dilemma of black manhood in America.* New York: Simon & Schuster.

Neale, S. (2000). *Genre and Hollywood.* London, Routledge.

Patterson, J. (1993). *Along came a spider.* Boston: Little Brown.

Raper, A.F. (1969). *The tragedy of lynching.* New Jersey: Patterson Smith.

Tolnay, E. and Beck, E.M. (1995). *A festival of violence: An analysis of southern lynching, 1882-1930.* Chicago: University of Illinois Press.

Biography

Pearlie Strother-Adams is an associate professor in the Department of English and Journalism at Western Illinois University, Macomb. She is co-editor of *Dealing With Diversity II: The Anthology* (2008), second edition. Her research centers on representations of African American males in American media. She is also a freelance writer and is currently working on a book of short narratives that focus on her life in Selma, Alabama as a child of the civil rights movement.

The Other Brother

Kathy-Ann C. Hernandez, Ph.D.
Eastern University

In 2008, Cable News Network (CNN) aired a special entitled "Black in America." This series of documentaries explored the experiences of Black men, women, and their families. Over the course of a few nights, Americans heard and saw gripping personal accounts and commentary on the myriad challenges Black people face in the United States: rates of HIV/AIDS infection, single parenthood, incarceration, and disparities in education, career and economic achievement. In one of the most poignant vignettes, the narrator, Soledad O'Brien, recounted the experiences of two brothers, Dr. Michael Eric Dyson and Everett Dyson. Both men grew up in the same household; however, their life trajectories are vastly different. Dr. Michael Dyson is a minister, author, intellect, and a onetime professor at the University of Pennsylvania, now employed at Georgetown University. His brother Everett, a past drug dealer and admitted pariah in his community, is serving a life sentence for a murder he insists he did not commit. The irony is gripping as Dyson writes: "One may teach, as I did for years, at Penn. The other, like my brother, could be locked away in the pen" (2008, p.1). What is striking in this story is the juxtaposition of two different life paths for two very similar Black men. What is troubling is that the prevalent narrative surrounding Black males in the United States is consistent with Everett's story.

As an educational psychologist, my research has been focused on understanding some of the factors affecting the achievement of Black males[1] in school and society. However, my continuing immersion with the literature on this topic has been paralleled with a growing frustration with how Black men are pathologized in academic and social discourse. The central motivation for this essay, therefore, is to highlight the importance of creating counter narratives to the dominant storyline—to tell the story of the other brother.

In this essay, I advance a case for research that targets this subset of the Black male population. First, I begin by reviewing several challenges affecting Black men, then I critique theoretical constructions of Black masculinity that have historically undergirded research relevant to Black males, but yet do not adequately represent the experiences of Black men and in particular religious/spiritual[3] Black men. I trace the historical importance of the church in the Black community and the potential it has to promote more positive definitions of masculinity. Finally, I present an agenda for research that includes the religious/spiritual socio-identity of Black men, and I discuss the potential benefits of this line of research for the academic and Black community.

Challenges Affecting Black Males

Black masculinity is scrutinized in academic and public circles. Attention is focused on possible linkages to constructions of manhood and significant social challenges affecting this population. Evidence of these challenges is certainly not lacking. Black males are the leading perpetrators and victims of homicides, violent acts, and related criminal activities (Skolnick & Currie, 1994). They make up a large percentage of the prison population; since 2001, one in six Black men has been incarcerated (Mauer & King, 2007). According to the Center for Disease Control, Black men are also contracting HIV/AIDS in alarming numbers. For the period 2001 to 2005, of the estimated 184,991 newly reported cases, Blacks represented 51% of such diagnoses with Black male adults accounting for 55, 267 [61%] new cases, and Black adult females only 35,160 [39%] (Durant, McDavid, Hu, & Sullivan, 2007).

In schools, the portrait is also very bleak. Black males are vulnerable to a variety of negative consequences including academic failure, special education assignment, under-representation in Advance Placement Programs, suspensions, expulsions and violence (Brown & Davis, 2000; Hernandez & Davis, 2009; National Center for Education Statistics, [NCES], 1998; Roderick, 2003). Alarming rates of school attrition, poor academic performance, and lower college enrollment numbers relative to Black females suggest a devaluing of the importance of conventional learning relative to fulfilling their roles in society as Black men.

Cultural messages about Black men, informed by negative portrayals of them in the media, follow them outside the classroom door and affect their identity formation (Hooks, 2004). Their manhood is linked to the adjectives violent, disrespectful, unintelligent, hyper-sexualized, and threatening (Young, 2003). Their language, demeanors and dispositions are often interpreted as defiant, aggressive, and intimidating. They are the "bad boys" in schools (Ferguson, 2000), the aggressive and defiant athletes in national sports, and the "pimps" and "players" sung of in gangster rap. These word images have become iconic of Black masculinity.

What is it about Black manhood that is linked to a vulnerability to negative social outcomes? Theorists have posited that individuals are products of the ecological niches they occupy (Bronfenbrenner, 1989, Vygotsky, 1978). Ethnic or gender identification is therefore a function of social context—home, school, community, religious and the wider cultural milieu. Unfortunately, for many African Americans, these contexts can be categorized as impoverished and reflective of lingering structural inequities—22.7 % of African Americans live below the poverty line, compared with a mere 7.8% of Caucasians (U.S. Census Bureau, 2002). In 1987, Wilson declared that the circumstances in which disadvantaged children are socialized have significant impacts on their development. They are products of the spaces they occupy. Religious and/or spiritual contexts are salient spaces for consideration in understanding Black males.

Religious or Spiritual Context

Arguably, religious involvement is not synonymous with spirituality. In a study conducted by Kunjufu (1994), Black men were careful to distinguish between religiosity and spirituality. Spirituality was viewed as a personal belief in a higher power and a desire to do the right thing, whereas religiosity involved affiliation with a particular denomination. According to the former definition, several of these men described themselves as spiritual.

There appears to be concurrence in social science circles, that religion represents "a fixed system of ideas and ideological commitments that "fail to represent the dynamic personal element in human piety" (Wuff, 1996, p. 46). On the other hand, spirituality "is increasingly used to refer to the personal, subjective side of religious experience" (Hill & Pargament, 2003, p.64). Taylor, Chatters and Levin (2005), who have been prolific researchers on the topic of religion in the lives of African Americans, suggest that definitions of religion conform to the biases of specific disciplines and contribute to definitional ambiguity. There is growing empirical and anecdotal evidence that religiosity and spiritual are not discrete but overlapping constructs (Moberg, 1990).

Research targeted at this area must of necessity clarify this overlap. In this paper, I use the term "religiosity/spirituality" broadly acknowledging that individuals may choose to express their spirituality by affiliation with a particular religious denomination or maintain spiritual connection to a higher being outside of traditional church affiliation.

Theorizing Black Masculinity

Connell's social theory of gender (2005), specifically hegemonic masculinity is among one of the most well cited in explicating issues surrounding Black masculinity. According to Connell, masculinity is negotiated in practice based on factors such as context, race, class and generation. He suggests that there is no one blueprint for masculinity or femininity. Instead, it is more appropriate to speak of masculinities/femininities. Hegemonic masculinity embodies

> the currently most honored way of being a man, it [requires] all other men to position themselves in relation to it, and it ideologically [legitimates] the global

95

subordination of women to men (Connell & Messerschmidt, 2005, p. 832).

In Western societies like the United States, this definition of masculinity is congruent with what the majority culture values—whiteness, heterosexuality, marriage, authority and physical toughness (Giddens, 2006). In the purest sense of Connell's theory, as Demetriou (2001) has noted, hegemonic masculinity is at the center and masculinities such as gay and effeminate masculinities are subordinate to this ideal, while other forms like working class and Black masculinities are marginalized.

In spite of substantial criticism of this theory (Demetriou, 2001, Wetherell & Edley, 1999), it remains one of the most cogent and comprehensive explanations of the social construction of gender. Yet, even as Connell and Messerschmidt (2005) have rebutted such criticisms, they acknowledge that hegemonic masculinity continues to reformulate in a given historical context. Moreover, since its emergence in the research world (Carrigan, Connell, & Lee 1985), it has expanded in view of empirical findings. Several international studies have illustrated diverse forms of masculinity among Chileans (Valdés & Olavarría, 1998), Japanese (Ishii-Kuntz, 2003), and Mexicans (Gutmann, 1996). There is every reason to expect that it will continue to evolve.

I argue, therefore, that the application of this theory to constructions of Black masculinity provides unique opportunities to explicate how it functions in the lives of African American men who subscribe to a religious/spiritual way of life. Connell's description of masculinity as a purely social construct fails to address the contribution of absolute religious/spiritual standards in the formation of gender ideal. While his view provides a strong foundation for understanding the fluidity of gender from a social constructivist perspective, it negates the Christian worldview. For many Protestant denominations, there is a God-given mandate on gender to which members are expected to conform as part of a larger cosmic struggle in which Christian theology is based. For example, Van Leeuwen (2003) argues that gender construct is spiritually rooted in God-given mandates to the first inhabitants of the earth. She notes further

> gender is never a completely social construct. At the very least it must cooperate with physical and reproductive differences between the sexes in which people carry out the cultural mandate (p. 46).

How hegemony plays out in this context and how it substantiates/ confounds/counteracts with popular definitions is a salient line of investigation for further research.

In addition, although Connell and others have argued elsewhere that masculinity is continually in flux, reconfiguring, transforming itself, the common ideal of hegemonic masculinity is based on a Eurocentric, Western, populous perspective. From this point of reference, the "cultural ideal" of hegemonic masculinity within the United States context is reflective of the dominant White[2] culture, what it values and what it idealizes. Hegemonic masculinity acknowledges the significance of context on constructions of masculinity, but research relevant to construction of Black masculinity against the background of the sociological and historical US context is still relatively scarce.

Finally, recent attempts at provoking deeper inquiry into more nuanced understandings of Black masculinity have emerged from the field of literary studies. In the book *Black Masculinity and the U.S. South: From Uncle Tom to Gangsta.* (2007), Richardson, presents a well-constructed critique of "the continued privileging of the urban within narratives of black masculinity in African American popular culture" (p. 205). In *Our Living Manhood: Literature, Black Power, and Masculine Ideology*, Murray (2007) advocates for a movement away from monolithic constructions of the lives of African American men to an appreciation for the dynamic "living manhood" that is continually evolving.

For these reasons, there is scope to advance deeper examinations of the construction of gender that account for religious/spiritual affiliation and constructions of masculinity, and more specifically as it applies to one of the most vulnerable populations in the United States—Black males.

Understanding Black Masculinities

In spite of the increasing focus on Black men in public circles, some ambiguity exists in understanding them from a gendered perspective. Superficial analyses of the lives of Black men is often flawed in one of two respects: (a) They presuppose a congruity with a Euro-Americanized definition of manhood as a result of the theoretical assumptions underlying measures of masculinity, and/or (b) They define Black masculinity as a singular construct consistent with the "Strong Black Man" of Black Power days or the iconic "Tyrone" (Hopkinson & Moore, 2006) of recent hip-hop fame. Additionally, given the richness of the Black US cultural context, it is regrettable that the salience of religious/spiritual context in constructions of Black masculinity has not received more attention. Unfortunately, these approaches do scant justice to providing an accurate explanation of Black manhood.

Theoretical Assumptions Underlying Measures of Masculinity

Several early attempts to measure masculinities in social science research have been based on the assumption that masculinity is a single construct that involves inherent traits that transcend cultural diversity. In the 1970s, the focus was on explicating the margins of male sex roles. Euro-American bias was evident in the phraseology that labeled these roles as true of "traditional American Masculinity." Masculine ideology was the belief system that directed the roles of traditional American men and was defined as "endorsement and internalization of cultural belief systems about masculinity and male gender, rooted in the structural relationships between the sexes" (Pleck, Sonenstein, & Ku, 1993, p. 88). In the 1980s, the focus shifted to an understanding of how men negotiated the burden of conformity to masculine norms. Gender role strain (SRS; Pleck, 1981) or the closely aligned gender role conflict scales assessed the level of negative psychological and physiological stress that accompanied men's attempts to meet societal male role expectations (Good, Wallace, & Borst, 1994).

Finally, in the 1990s, attention turned towards understanding masculinity from a historical and contextual perspective. Whereas the preceding two decades focused almost exclusively on masculinity as an attribute residing in individuals, the present emphasis has been to acknowledge both the plurality of the construct and its context specificity (Smiler, 2004). Instead of the singular term, *masculinity*, the term *masculinities* was used to include Jocks, Sensitive Men, and Gay Men, and Black men (Connell, 2005; Kimmel, 1997; Messner, 1992). Conformity to masculine norms may therefore differ by group and by context. Pleck *et al.* (1993) have suggested that the behavior of males is not a function of "their male role identity, or level of masculine traits, but because of the conception of masculinity they internalize from their culture" (pp. 114-115). Hence, masculinity ideology may differ significantly for African American men relative to Caucasian men.

Several studies have reported cultural differences in masculine ideology (Cazenave, 1984; Levant & Majors, 1997; Thompson, Grisani, & Pleck, 1985). For example, Cazenave (1984) found that white-collar African American men placed greater stress on competitiveness, aggression, protection of family, success, and independence relative to Euro-Americans. They were also more likely to endorse gentleness of expression in males, warmth and standing up for one's beliefs. Other studies have found that Black males appear to have less rigid conceptions of masculine and feminine roles relative to White males (Albert & Porter, 1988; Smith & Milarsky, 1985). Hunter & Davis' 1994 qualitative analysis of manhood as defined by 32 Black men revealed a multidimensional construct comprising four major themes: (a) self-determination and accountability, (2) family, (3) pride, and (4) spirituality and humanism. The priority placed on these attributes varied by occupational status.

The Evolution of Black Masculinities

Black masculinity is not monolithic. Yet, if one were to judge from the pervasive iconography, the converse is true. Black men are embodiments of physical prowess and "a reigning symbol of aggressive American manliness" (Ross, 1998, p. 599). Without the juxtaposition of adequate alternates, the imagery of the "Strong Black Man" by default becomes the sole narrative. This depiction owes much to the historical antecedents affecting Black life in American society as it does to the media's penchant of problematizing Black men. The current focus on Black men "in crisis" is, at the core, a resurgence of an old theme. Writers have long considered how struggles for emancipation, equal rights, and the residual effects of slavery have created unique and potent interconnections of race, class, and gender within the Black community (Boyd, 1997; Newton; 2005; Ross, 1998).

In her book *From Panthers to Promise Keepers,* Judith Newton (2005) describes major influences and icons in given time periods that impacted the social construction of Black masculinity during the 1960s and 70s. In the 1960s, with the onset of the Black Power movement, Malcolm X became the embodiment of Black manhood characterized by the commitment to a communal struggle juxtaposed with militancy (Cade, 1970). In the 1970s, Huey Newton extended Malcolm X's platform through the Black Panther Party, but undermined its effectiveness by his own personal struggles. There was a clash between "his investment in familial, brotherly, communal ties and his serve-the-people ideals" and "his individualistic, violence-prone street masculinity" (Newton, 2005, p. 66). His eventual demise is a tragic account of drug addiction, violence, corruption and imprisonment. However, in the 1980s, a more diluted version of the masculine ideal of the Black man committed to elevating the race was restored.

Boyd (1997) presents three types of Black Manhood that have emerged from the 1980s onward: the *race man*, the New Black Aesthetic, and niggaz. He defines *race men* as individuals "who, through their efforts, exemplified excellence in the interest of . . . uplifting the race" (Boyd, 1997, p. 18). Black role models personified in the likes of Bill Cosby. Their persona makes Blackness more palatable because it represents assimilation into mainstream White culture and a simultaneous nullification of negative stereotypes. As the "race man" imagery began to decline in significance, a new expression of Black masculinity has surfaced—the New Black Aesthetic (NBA). Trey Ellis (1989), who coined the term, describes them as "cultural mulattoes," individuals educated by a multi-racial mix of cultures and able to "navigate easily in the White world" (p. 20).This is the generation that has transcended the Civil Rights Era. They know the history of slavery and Jim Crow but have not experienced this type of direct racism. By virtue of access to equal rights fought for and won by their forefathers, they have been able to attend elite universities and fraternize with the best of society. Schooled in the history of their people and possessing the intellectual skills and connections, they are able to promote the Black aesthetic in newer, less militant platforms (Boyd, 1997). Barrack Obama's bid for the 2008 presidential election is ample evidence of the emergence of this growing stratum in American society.

For the masses, however, another definition of manhood exists. Boyd (1997) labels this the "niggaz" subgroup—men who embrace anti-assimilation ideologies. Robin Kelly (1994) acknowledges that class is the defining characteristic separating NBAs from niggaz. Niggaz link "their identity to the hood instead of simply skin color" (p. 210). A subgroup comprises Blacks who have transcended poverty, but choose to identify with the culture of the "hood." For the latter group, access to wealth and the upper class lifestyle as successful athletes or entertainers frees them from obligations to conform to White mainstream culture. Boyd (1997) suggests that Charles Barkley is a member of this group. In a 1992 interview, Barkley described himself as "a 90's nigga" free to do as he pleased. These men "[defy] both the decorum of social acceptability and overtly political nature of the new Black aesthetic." They reject mainstream values and "not only [are] uneducated, but [see] value only in being educated in the streets and the hard-core urban environment that [they exist] in" (Boyd, 1997, p. 33).

Hip-hop has surfaced as the medium for promoting "niggaz" rhetoric. Price (2005) writes that "Black males are at the center of hip hop" (p. 60). This genre defines them and describes with great detail how they should act. Through the lyrical presentations, male-to-male relationships are portrayed as confrontational, disputes are best settled through violence, athleticism is a way of proving one's manhood, and males are sexual subjects and women the objects of "booty calls." In fact, in many rap videos, it is a common gesture for men to hold their genital area "as a gesture of sexual prowess disrespecting women as sexual objects" (Price, 2005, p. 60).

Prior to the election of President Barack Obama, the first Black American president, this is the definition of manhood that is most often depicted on the evening news. It is an expression of manhood that is perceived as aimless, dangerous, and self-destructive (Kunjufu, 2004). Instead of being the strong presence in the struggle for Black group enfranchisement, it has become a medium of self-expression captured in the imagery of hyper-aggressiveness, hyper-sexuality, excessive emphasis on appearance and wealth, and the absence of personal accountability birthed in the struggles of the Black urban underclass (Anderson, 1990; Oliver, 1984).

Boyd's 1997 categorization of Black manhood is an attempt to add clarity to a complex construct. What this classification demonstrates quite well is that constructions of Black manhood evolve in response to the ecological zeitgeist and the complex interplay of personality, possession, and power. The inherent weakness in a neat classification system is that it cannot adequately account for multiple configurations where individuals straddle more than one category simultaneously or at different times in their developmental experience. More specifically, the voices of religious/spiritual Black men and other sub-groups are not well represented in this paradigm.

The Role of Religion in the Lives of Black Males

Religion has been a central pillar in the African American community. In a 1976 publication, the United Methodist Church Board of Discipleship recognized religion as "the organizing principle of black experience in America" (p. 57). A National Survey of Black Americans (NSBA) revealed that religion features prominently in the everyday lives of African Americans (Levin, Taylor, & Chatters, 1995).

In spite of the significant role of religion in the lives of African Americans, participation is structured along gender lines. African American females are perceived within many families as the progenitors of religious life and ethos. They report greater church involvement and ascribe greater importance than males to the importance of religion (Mattis, 2005, p. 195). In many households, females are the ones who attend church on behalf of members of their extended families. The exact nature of Black male involvement with the church has been the topic of considerable debate in the academic community. One possible source of misinterpretation in understanding their involvement has been cited by Levin, Taylor and Chatters (1995). Since research conducted on African Americans church involvement relies heavily on self-reported data, present calculations provide a description of self-reported male involvement and should not be construed as evidence that Black females are more religious than males. However, such reports have often been coupled with anecdotal data regarding male presence in the church.

In his book, *Adam Where are You? Why Most Black Men Don't Go to Church*, Kunjufu (1994) recounts 21 reasons articulated by a group of Black men regarding why they do not attend church. A prevalent theme among this group of respondents was that church involvement was incompatible with constructions of Black masculinity. They questioned the relevance of "White Blonde, blue-eyed [images] of Jesus proudly displayed in the church sanctuary" (Kunjufu, 1994, p. 61). Others spoke of the emotionality of the worship experience involving "hollering" and "dancing down the aisle." In their view, this explains in part why churches are attracting more women than men "because woman [sic] are emotional, and brothers are logical and rational" (Kunjufu, 1994, p.63). The demands of the church regarding sexuality and fidelity were also sources of contention. Men questioned why the church should make demands on them to be monogamous. They also described the church as a feminized space composed mainly of "women, elders, children, and sissies." The few men who were involved in church, they characterized as effeminates and not ideal models of Black masculinity. One man explained it this way:

That's why I let my girls go to church but not my boys. I want my boys to be like me. I want my boys to be strong. I want my boys to be macho. I don't want them crying (Kunjufu, 1994, p. 67).

These men were also careful to distinguish between religiosity and spirituality. Spirituality was viewed as a personal belief in a higher power and a desire to do the right thing, whereas religiosity involved affiliation with a particular denomination. According to the former definition, several of these men self-identified as spiritual.

Religious/Spiritual Constructions of Black Masculinity

Historical accounts of masculinity within the Christian church are reflective of dominant Euro-Americanized perspectives. Even though African Americans were at the margins of Christian discourse, tensions in explicating the relationship between Christianity and spirituality has influenced how it is constructed in the Black community. In an article entitled, "Is it Manly to be a Christian? The Debate in Victorian and Modern America," Kirkley (1996) outlines two prominent views on this topic. On one hand, men who subscribed to atheism believed that Christianity stagnated rather than nurtured masculine fortitude because it dictated how men should be and robbed them of independent, free thought. However, others viewed religious affiliation as the ideal setting for men to achieve true manhood by reclaiming their rightful headship and reestablishing the authentic "masculine, militant, warlike" ethos to a numerically female dominated Christian church (Smith, 1913, p. 70). Echoes of these sentiments are present today in groups such as the Men's Studies in Religion Group (MSRG) and Promise Keepers (PK) respectively (Kirkley, 1996).

Promise Keepers (PK) was established in 1990 as a reaction to growing concerns that American men were being feminized. The goal of the movement was to empower men to reclaim their leadership roles in society. From its early beginnings as a "hard-boiled" version of masculinity when Tony Evans (1994) charged men to take back the leadership roles in their homes, PK has evolved to a "soft-boiled" version of its former self. Advocates now challenge masculine norms by embracing male-male intimacy, holding hands, singing and sharing deeply at men's events (Heath, 2003). However, like earlier manifestations of men's movements, PK comprises a predominantly White, middle class membership (Newton, 2005).

Black men who subscribe to a religious or spiritual lifestyle have often found community in other efforts to mobilize them in the quest for a redefinition of masculinity. Under the leadership of Minister Louis Farrakhan, one of the most conspicuous of these events was the Million Man March in Washington D.C in 1995. Farrakhan urged men to march in the spirit of "atonement and reconciliation." The aim was to "reverse the ugly look of Black men throughout the world by giving the world a positive look at militant, dedicated, sober, determined Black men" (Farrakhan, 1995, p. 65).

Farrakhan, leader of the reestablished Nation of Islam (NOI), which was originally founded in the 1930's, has earned a place as one of the prominent forces mobilizing Black men in spiritual constructions of manhood. In 2002, it was estimated that 30,000 to 70,000 of 2.5 million African American Muslims belonged to the Nation of Islam (Wood, 2002). Contrary to dominant social models of masculinity, NOI men commit to a lifestyle of morality, personal decorum, modesty, mutual respect, and discipline in dress and deportment. In keeping with traditional Muslim teachings, members are expected to abstain from the consumption of pork, alcohol, drugs, or tobacco, and to commit to healthy diet and physical fitness.

Other Black religious leaders have sought to mobilize men under a Christian definition of manhood. Reverend T.D. Jakes has become one of the leading black neo-Pentecostal televangelists impacting Black religious culture. Although a strong advocate for empowerment of women, Jakes also teaches an essentialist approach to gender. Lee (2005) defines this approach as a belief in the "essence of being male and female that does not vary from society to society but that it defines the very nature, purpose, and function of each gender" (p. 130). Jakes's view is that God created men and women to fulfill different functions. He (1997) writes:

One of the great differences between men and women is rooted in this: Man had position with God before he had relationship with another human being. Woman was birthed in a relationship. We see that men are positional and women are relational. (p. 45)

He suggests further that distinctions between men and women are God-given after creation. Hence, men are naturally driven to seek status and power and women to be focused on relationship issues. Lee (2005) observes that Jakes's messages on gender "convey the idea that God made men to be strong and aggressive and women to be tender" (p. 131). A strong critic of effeminacies, Jakes asserts, however, that it might or might not be reflective of homosexuality. Instead, he argues that effeminate conduct is a sin and a misrepresentation of true masculinity conduct including homosexuality (Jakes, 1997, p. 131). Consistent with a conservative Protestant platform, Jakes also subscribes to the view that the leadership role of men within the home context is a God-given responsibility.

Other Christian scholars offer a different interpretation of gender roles. Van Leeuwen (2003) advocates the use of new terminologies to explicate the spiritual root of gender constructs. She uses the term "manhood" and "womanhood" as opposed to masculinity and femininity to suggest that these are "neither fixed blueprints for behavior nor arbitrary social constructions, but something in between. She argues that when God created the man and the woman, he charged them *both* with the same responsibilities. Both the man and the woman were given the responsibility for "dominion" and "community", responsibility for power and for relationships. Moreover, the powers of manhood and womanhood were perverted by the biblical account of a Fall when the couple sinned (Van Leewen, 2003, p. 46). Hence, God pronounced a curse on the pair when he said to Eve, "Your desire shall be for your husband, and he shall rule over you" (Genesis 3: 16).

A literal interpretation of this pronouncement as explained by Jakes suggests that God rescinded the original responsibility he had given to the woman. However, Van Leeuwen asserts that God's pronouncement was descriptive rather than prescriptive of the dreadful consequences of sin for both the man and the woman.

> More specifically postfall man is continually tempted to turn legitimate, God-imaging dominion into domination, and to impose it in illegitimate ways on the earth and on other men but also on woman, his God-given partner" (p. 47).

The Christian imperative is, therefore, for more egalitarian relations between the sexes.

These two schools of thought—a conservative and more liberal interpretation—of a God-given mandate on gender exists in nuanced iterations in Protestant churches throughout America. Within the Black community, they metamorphose into distinct teachings that prescribe expected behaviors

Advancing a Research Agenda

The critical challenges affecting Black males in schools and society demand a research agenda that is inclusive of research areas that have the potential to change the prevalent script. The Black church has long functioned as a respite and a space that has nurtured and effected significant social change in American society. In spite of the potency of this connection, there remains a paucity of studies investigating the impact of religious/spiritual affiliation on social outcomes in this population.

In this essay, I have explored the inadequacies of current theoretical understanding of masculinity in representing the experiences of Black men who occupy religious/spiritual spaces. Moreover, the prevalence of such theoretical considerations in social science research has served a dubious purpose of silencing the voices of these Black brothers, while simultaneously endorsing research narrowly focused on privileging problems associated with constructions of Black masculinity. Advancing a research agenda on this salient topic is relevant for theoretical, methodological and practical considerations relevant to this group.

First, current explanations of gender construction, such as the view articulated by Connell (2005), need to be expanded to adequately explain constructions of Black masculinity. Connell's theory presents a macro view of how gender is constructed for a hypothetical typical man (non-racial/cultural, non-age specific, non-religious/spiritual, etc.). Such a skeletal framework is a valuable foundation on which to build a living theory that is responsive to change. Research is needed to tease out how and if it holds its shape as a valid explanation for how Black Masculinity is constructed as other researchers have done for other cultural/ethnic groups (Gutmann, 1996; Valdés & Olavarría, 1998; Ishii-Kuntz, 2003). Additionally, the absolute views of gender ideal prevalent in Black Protestant churches and those prescribed by the Nation of Islam followers, which run counter culture to populous definitions, call into question the validity of understanding gender from a purely social constructivist perspective. How do these Black men negotiate masculinity ideology prescribed by their faith and more populous definitions? How do these negotiations impact their faith and life experiences? Within their spiritual/religious context, which masculinities emerge as dominant and which are subordinate? How do these negotiations mirror/contradict similar hegemonies in the public sphere? These are important questions deserving further investigation.

Secondly, this field of inquiry can do much to advance clearer understandings of the two important constructs in this alliance—Black masculinity and religiosity/spirituality. Current understandings of masculinity have emerged from a long history. Yet, researchers intent on studying masculinity among Black males have limited choices of instruments that are responsive to cultural/ethnic distinctions. Masculinity is not an acontextual construct. In spite of ample evidence supporting this view, there remains a paucity of instrumentation sensitive to cultural/ ethnic differences. Doss (1998) has noted that qualitative studies have not been effective in inspiring culturally sensitive quantitative instrumentation to assess masculine ideology. In response to this need, he created the Multicultural Masculinity Ideology Scale. The instrument was designed based on reviews of psychological and sociology literature on Hispanic, African American and Anglo-American masculinity. The construction, validation and use of similar psychometrically sound instruments is needed.

Similarly, attempts to quantify religious or spiritual experience continue to pose a challenge for social science researchers. Early unidimensional measures have been critiqued because they relied almost exclusively on public behaviors in traditional settings (e.g., church attendance and participation), but did not address more subjective experiences (e.g., private devotional practices and prayer). New multidimensional measures of religiosity/spirituality attempt to cover the breadth of experiences by comprising both behavioral and subjective indices (Taylor, Chatters, & Levin, 2004). Behavioral components tap participation both in public and private or church related activities; they comprise elements like denominational affiliation, religious service attendance, prayer, meditations, and devotional reading. Subjective components "include attitudes, experiences, self-perceptions, and attributions that involve religious spiritual content, (e.g., religious identity, feelings of closeness to God)" (p. 30). One such measure is the Brief Multidimensional Measure of Religiousness/Spirituality (Fetzer, 1999). However, there is need for further inquiry into the exact relationships between these constructs to provide viable options for disaggregating the salience of each to targeted outcome measures.

Thirdly, this line of research has potential for understanding the importance of a faith component in intervention programs targeted at Black males. In the past, political sensitivities relevant to separation of church and state in federally funded programs have dampened interest in the topic. However, continued research has been instrumental in distinguishing between religiosity and spirituality making it easy to maintain this separation. In recent years, the proliferation of faith-based initiatives has propelled interest in religiosity and/or spirituality as a viable construct that can influence program outcomes. As such, more research can provide substantive evidence for the viability of the faith life experience as a suitable alternative or salient composition in intervention programs targeted at this population. This line of research has the potential to provide useful data to effect positive changes. Even from a purely social science perspective, the importance of spiritual affiliation as a means of social control is well established in research and is based on a perspective that religious/spiritual beliefs provide a foundation for moral behavior (Chadwick, 1993).

Finally, within the Black community, the church has long functioned as an institution that can be a potent force in effecting social change. Research that explores challenges and opportunities that can position the church to reclaim its social responsibility to the Black community, by creating safe/comfortable spaces where Black men can learn alternative constructions of masculinity that are sensitive to Black culture, would be invaluable. We need to give voice to the men who occupy religious/spiritual spaces, whether it is within the walls of a church or their unique spiritual context. There are different narratives concerning Black males other than the prevalent ones seen on the evening news. I challenge researchers to advance research on behalf of these other brothers.

Notes

1. The term "African American Males" refers to American born males who self-identify as African Americans. However, one of the methodological challenges related to studies of African American males is that such studies invariably include Black males from other geographic regions who have migrated to the United States, including Africa and the Caribbean. In this paper, I use the term "Black" as an inclusive adjective representing African Americans and other sub-groups.
2. As I explain later in this essay, religiosity is not synonymous with spirituality. However, throughout this paper, I use "religious/spiritual" as an inclusive term for males who may self-identify as one or the other.
3. The terms White and European are used interchangeably in this paper.

Bibliography

Albert, A. A. & Porter, J. R. (1988). Children's gender-role stereotypes: A sociological investigation of psychological models. *Sociological Forum, 3*, 184-210.

Anderson, E. (1990). *Streetwise: Race, Class, and Change in an Urban Community.* Chicago: University Press.

Boyd, T. (1997). *Am I Black Enough for you? Popular Culture From the 'Hood and Beyond.* Bloomington, ID: Indiana University Press.

Bronfenbrenner, U. (1989). Ecological systems theory. *Annals of Child Development, 6,* 187-249.

Brown, M. C., & Davis, J. E. (2000). Black sons to mothers: Compliments, critiques, and challenges for cultural workers in education. New York: Peter Lang.

Cade, T. (Ed.). (1970). *The Black Woman: An Anthology.* New York: Signet.

Carrigan, T., Connell, R.W., & Lee. J.(1985). Toward a new sociology of masculinity. *Theory and Society, 14*(5), 551-604.

Cazenave, N. A. (1984). Race, socioeconomic status, and age: The social context of American Masculinity. *Sex Roles, 11,* 639-656.

Chadwick, B.A, & Top, B.L. (1993). Religiosity and Delinquency Among LSD Adolescents. *Journal of Scientific Studies of Religion, 32*(1), 51-67.

Connell, R. W. (2005). *Masculinities.* (2nd ed.). Cambridge: Polity Press.

Connell, R. W., & Messerschmidt (2005). Hegemonic Masculinity: Rethinking the Concept. *Gender and Society, 19*(6), 829-859.

Demetriou, D. Z. (2001). Connell's Concept of Hegemonic Masculinity: A Critique. *Theory and Society, 30,* 337-361.

Doss, B. D., (1998, May). The Multicultural Ideology Scale: Validation from Three Cultural Perspectives. *Sex Roles, 38,* (9-10*), 719-741.*

Durant, T., McDavid C., Hu, X., & Sullivan, P. (2007, April 18). Racial/Ethnic Disparities in Diagnoses of HIV/AIDS—33 States, 2001-2005, *The Journal of the American Medical Association., 297*(15), 1647-1649.

Dyson, M. E. (2008, July). Black in America 2: Commentary: Me and my brother and black America. (Retrieved November 25, 2009

from
http://www.cnn.com/2008/US/07/23/bia.michael.dyson/index.ht
ml

Ellis, T. (1985, May 15). The New Black Aesthetic. *Before Columbus Review*, 4, 23.

Evans, T. (1994). Spiritual Purity, In *Seven Promises of a Promise Keeper*. Colorado: Focus on the Family Publishing, p. 79.

Farrakhan, L. (1995). "A Call to March" *Emerge, 7*(1), 65-66.

Ferguson, A. A. (2000). *Bad boys: Public schools in the making of Black Masculinity (law, meaning and violence)*. Ann Arbor, MI: University of Michigan Press.

Fetzer Institute (1999). *Multidimensional measurement of religiosity/spirituality for use in health Research.* A report of the Fetzer Institute National Institute on Aging Working Group, Fetzer Institute.

Giddens, A. (2006). *Sociology* (5th ed.). Cambridge: Polity Press.

Good, G. E., Wallace, D. L., & Borst, T.S. (1994). Masculinity research: A review and critique. *Applied and Preventive Psychology, 3,* 3-14.

Gutmann, M. C. 1996. *The meanings of macho: Being a man in Mexico City*. Berkeley: University of California Press.

Heath, M. (2003). Soft-boiled Masculinity: Renegotiating Gender and racial Ideologies in the promise Keepers Movement. *Gender & Society, 17*(3), 423-444.

Hernandez. K., & Davis J.E. (2009). The Other Side of Gender: The Role of Masculinity in Teaching and Learning. In R. Milner (Ed.), *Possibilities of Diversity: A Guide for Practitioners* (pp. 17-30). Springfield, IL: C. Thomas Publishers.

Hill, P.C., & Pargament, K.I. (2003). Advances in the Conceptualization and Measurement of Religion and Spirituality: Implications for Physical and mental Health Research. *American Psychologist,58*(1), 64-74.

Hooks, B. (2004). *We Real Cool: Black men and masculinity*. New York: Routledge.

Hopkinson, N., & Moore, N.Y. (2006). *Deconstructing Tyrone: A New Look at Black Masculinity in the Hip-Hop Generation.* San Francisco: Cleis Press.

Hunter, G. A., & Davis, J. E. (1994). Constructing Gender: An exploration of Afro-American Men's Conceptualization of Manhood. *Gender and Society, 6*(3), 464-479.

Ishii-Kuntz, M. 2003. Balancing fatherhood and work: Emergence of diverse masculinities in contemporary Japan. In *Men and masculinities in contemporary Japan,* edited by J. E. Roberson and N. Suzuki. London: Routledge Curzon.

Jakes. T. D. (1997, 1993). *Woman Thou Art Loosed: Healing the Wounds of the Past.* Shippensburg, PA: Destiny Image.

Kelly, R. (1994). Kickin Reality, Kickin Ballistics: Gangsta Rap and Postindustrial Los Angeles. *In* D. Robin & G. Kelley (Eds.). *Race rebels: culture, Politics and Black Working Class.* New York: Free Press.

Kimmel, M. S. (1997). Masculinity as homophobia: Fear, shame, and silence in the construction of gender identity. In M. M. Gergen & S. N. Davis (Eds.), *Toward a new psychology of gender* (pp. 223-242). New York: Routledge.

Kirkley, E. A. (1996). Is it Manly to be a Christian? The Debate in Victorian and Modern America. In S. Boyd, W. M. Longwood, & M. W. Muesse (Eds.). *Redeeming Men* (pp. 80-88). Louisville: Westminster John Knox Press.

Kunjufu, J. (1994). *Adam! Where Are You?: Why Most Black Men Don't Go to Church.* USA: African American Images.

Kunjufu, J. (2004). *Countering the Conspiracy to Destroy Black Boys, Vols. 1-4.* USA: African American Images.

Lee, S. (2005). *T. D. Jakes: America's New Preacher.* New York: New York University Press.

Levant & R. F., & Majors, R. G. (1997). Masculinity Ideology among African American and European college women and men. *Journal of Gender, Culture, and Health, Z,* 33-43.

Levin, J., Taylor, R., & Chatters, L. (1995). A multidimensional measure of religious involvements for African Americans. *Sociological Quarterly, 36,* 157-173.

113

Mauer, M., & King, R. S. (2007). Uneven Justice: State By State By race and Ethnicity Rate of Incarceration. Washington, DC: The Sentencing Project: Research and Advocacy Reform.

Mattis, J. (2005) Religion in African American Life. In V.C. McLoyd, N. E. Hill, & K. A. Dodge (Eds.) *African American Family Life: Ecological and Cultural Diversity.* New York, NY: Guilford Press.

Messner, M. A. (1992). *Power at play: Sports and the problem of masculinity.* Boston: Beacon Press.

Moberg, D. O. (1990). Religion and aging. In K. F. Ferraro (Ed.) *Gerontology: Perspectives and issues* (pp. 179-205). New York: Springer.

Murray, R. (2007). *Our Living Manhood: Literature, Black Power, and Masculine Ideology.* Philadelphia: University of Pennsylvania Press.

National Center for Education Statistics. (1998). *The Condition of Education 1998.* Washington, DC: US Department of Education.

Newton, J. (2005). *From Panthers to Promise Keepers: Rethinking the Men's Movement.* Lanham, MD: Rowan & Littlefield.

Oliver, W. (1984). Black males and the tough guy image: A dysfunctional compensatory adaptation. *Western Journal of Black Studies, 8,*199-203.

Pleck, J. H. (1981). *The myth of masculinity.* Cambridge, MA: MIT Press.

Pleck, J. H., Sonenstein, F. L., & Ku, L. C. (1993). Masculinity ideology and its correlates. In S Oskamp & M. Costanzo (Eds.) *Gender issues in social psychology* (pp. 85-110). Newbury Park, CA: Sage.

Price, R. J. (2005). Hegemony, Hope and the Harlem Renaissance: Taking Hip Hop Culture Seriously. *Convergence, XXXVIII* (2): 55-64.

Richardson, R. (2007). Black Masculinity and the U.S. South: From Uncle Tom to Gangsta. Athens: University of Georgia Press.

Roderick, M. (2003). What's happening to the boys? Early high school experience and school outcomes among African

American male adolescents in Chicago. *Urban Education, 38,* 538-607.

Ross, M. B. (1998) In search of Black men's masculinities. *Feminist Studies, 24*(3), 599-626.

Skolnick, J. & E. Currie. (1994). *Crisis in American Institutions.* New York: Harper Collins.

Smiler, A. P. (2004). Thirty years after the discovery of gender: Psychological concepts and measures of masculinity – 1. *Sex Roles: A Journal of Research, 50*(1/2), 15-26.

Smith, F. B. (1913). *A Man's Religion.* New York, Association.

Smith, P. A., & Milarsky, E. (1985). Empirically derived conceptions of femaleness and maleness: A current view. *Sex Roles, 12,* 313-319.

Taylor, R., Chatters, L., & Levin, J. (2004). *Religion in the Lives of African Americans: Social, Psychological, and Health, Perspectives.* Thousand Oaks: Sage.

Thompson, E. H., Jr., Grisani, C., & Pleck, J. H. (1985). Attitudes toward the male role and their correlates. *Sex Roles, 13,* 413-427.

United Methodist Church Board of Discipleship. (1976). *Ethnic minorities in the United Methodist Church.* Nashville, TN: Discipleship Resources.

United States Bureau of Census. (2002). *Table 1. People and families in poverty by selected characteristics: 2000 and 2001.* Retrieved June 29, 2007, from http://www.census.gov/hhes/www/poverty/poverty01

Valdés, T., & Olavarría. J. (Eds.). (1998). Ser hombre en Santiago de Chile: A pesar de todo, un mismo modelo. In *Masculinidades y equidad de género en América Latina,* Santiago, Chile: FLACSO/UNFPA.

Van Leeuwen, M.S. (2003). Fathers and Sons: In Search of a New Masculinity. Leicester: Inter-Varsity.

Vygotsky, L. S. (1978). *Mind in society: The development of higher psychological processes.* Cambridge, MA: Harvard University Press.

Wilson, W. J. (1987). *The Truly Disadvantaged: The Inner City, the Underclass, and Public Policy.* Chicago: University of Chicago Press.

Wetherell, M., & Edley, N. (1999). Negotiating hegemonic masculinity: Imaginary positions and psycho-discursive practices. *Feminism and Psychology 9*(3), 335-56.

Wuff, D.M. (1997). *Psychology of religion: Classic and contemporary* (2nd ed.). New York: Wiley.

Young, A. (2003). The minds of marginalized Black men: Making sense of mobility, opportunity, and future life chances. Princeton, NJ: Princeton University Press.

Biography

Kathy-Ann C. Hernandez is Associate Professor of Educational Psychology and Assessment and the Director of Research for the Loeb School of Education at Eastern University. Her research is focused on the Black Diaspora and the salience of race/ethnicity, gender and class in identity formation, and social and academic outcomes. She is coauthor of *Collaborative Autoethnography* (forthcoming in 2011, with Heewon Chang and Faith Wambura Ngunjiri).

My Experiences as a Community College President

Ralph Soney, Ed. D.
President, Roanoke-Chowan Community College

A veteran higher education administrator who happened to be a person of color once told me that her dilemma as she pursued a career in higher education was to determine whether she would be better off combating the dehumanizing effects of racism or the contradictory dilemma associated with reverse racism, which she called "niggerism." I was immediately drawn to the analogy and identified with her statement in a way that is powerful and captivating. Her words have given me a multitude of opportunities for reflection as I have tried to ponder the experiences that I have had as a black male in higher education administration and subsequently as a community college president.

I am not sure how common my experiences are to those brothers, though few as they may be, that serve as CEOs of colleges and universities across our country. Community colleges ironically are often cast as institutions that give access to the socially disenfranchised. Though not a one hundred percent completely accurate generalization, it is accurate to say that the majority of enrollees at our community colleges have had life issues that are far more intense than the traditional university student. Given the fact that community colleges are often viewed as our nation's equivalent to educational Ellis Islands (George Vaughan's Poem), it stands to reason that the experience of leadership on the part of a CEO from a underrepresented group might provide some insight into something or at least a contribution to the zeitgeist. I am uncertain if mine does.

I am not sure about the degree to which my experiences as an African American CEO of a community college is predicated upon the fact that my school is in the south, in the State of North Carolina, which still manages to institutionalize racism despite claims of equal opportunity for employment upon virtually every job announcement it posts. It took me 23 years to become a president of a community college. I taught psychology and history for thirteen years before becoming the dean of a division of programs. After three successful years as a dean, I became the third African American to serve as the Chief Academic Officer of one of the 58 colleges within our system. After four years of successful service and noteworthy accomplishments as a chief academic officer, I had several unsuccessful attempts as an applicant for presidencies across our system. In actuality, in my state and the system that I have worked in and received several awards, I have made it to the interview process twice, one being for the position that I currently hold. Imagine my dismay as I often see colleagues with whom I worked who have less experience and half the educational attainment as myself interviewed and subsequently hired.

My next career move was to take a position at a larger institution as its chief academic officer. In some people's eyes, it may have been viewed as a lateral move; however, to the wise observer, it represented the equivalent of an intermediary step that many black people are obligated to get in order to prove that they are capable of handling certain professional responsibilities. Mind you, there is nothing that you will see listed in the section on qualifications for a position. The unwritten requirement to me as a black man was that I had to be a little bit better to get to the same spot as a white male.

After a period of noteworthy service in my second chief academic officer's position, I was encouraged to apply for a presidency at a particular college where the then president was being asked to leave. The college was in great distress financially and was missing the mark in every important measure as far as the leadership of the community college system was concerned. Perhaps the most sobering thing for me was the fact that the school's student population was mostly African American, as was the community that it served. I was sure that I could make a difference.

My mentors and supporters up until this point had been all "White Men of Good Will and Good Standing," as a prominent African

American figure had referred to their kind when asked, "What should a black person do to get ahead in higher education?" These supporters said things to me like, "If you go to this college and stay three to five years, you can write your ticket anywhere," and "You always want to go into a school that's doing poorly because the least thing you do will be brilliant by comparison." Unfortunately, about two years into my presidency, all of these "White Men of Good Will and Good Standing" either retired or died and took their influence with them.

Within two years into my first presidency, I found that the experience that I was having would not be duplicative of any that I observed among my white counterparts. Soon the collective memory of what this college had gone through and how much help it required to sustain it was gone. The newer leadership had neither the inclination nor the insight into the issues germane to my institution and its history. Ironically, my administration has been a textbook example of what a president is supposed to do to create stability and change. I believe that, if the same strategies were being employed by a white CEO, the experience would be far more fruitful for the college and the president. Indeed, the institution is stronger today than it was five years ago when I landed; however, the level of challenge, both internally and externally, have often caused serious moments of reflection.

Many years ago, as a sophomore at the university in an African American Literature class, I was introduced to Ralph Ellison's *Invisible Man*. If you would have asked me then if I would have any concept or understanding of what he was trying to say, I probably would have laughed. Ironically, my experience as the president of a community college has been much like what Ellison has described of the invisible man:

> I am an invisible man. No I am not a spook like those who haunted Edgar Allen Poe: Nor am I one of your Hollywood movie ectoplasms. I am a man of substance, of flesh and bone, fiber and liquids—and I might even be said to possess a mind. I am invisible, simply because people refuse to see me.

What I have found is that, even though as a black man, I have all the trappings of leadership and authority, as the president of a school, it becomes difficult for people to hear and see me. I am not sure if other brothers in similar roles would attest to this but it is often like the accomplishments and milestones are never noted nor acknowledged. I have found that, even among trustees and staff, there is a tendency to devalue and to overlook the intricacies of a black administration, even by blacks.

Though the comparison is almost humorous because the only thing that I share with President Obama is the word "president," I cannot help but see a true comparison of how people in this country react to leadership from a black man. Life as the president of a community college for me is analogous in many ways to what he is experiencing because few will ever allow him to get away from the fact that he is not just a man who happens to be in charge, he is a "black man" who is in charge. On some level, this very fact devalues and invades everything he does. It doesn't matter if those speaking are closeted bigots pretending to be modern or well-meaning people of color who over-identify with him. His actions will always be viewed in the context of his race. For me as the president of a community college, this is the context in which I live and work.

Biography

A native of Winston-Salem, North Carolina, Dr. Ralph Soney currently serves as the president of Roanoke-Chowan Community College in Ahoskie, North Carolina. He has 28 years of experience as a higher education professional. He has served in various capacities at five community colleges around North Carolina. He holds a Bachelor of Arts and a Master of Arts in Psychology (1980, 1991) as well as a Master of Arts in History (1983), all from Appalachian State University. He earned the Doctorate of Education in Adult and Community College Education from North Carolina State University (1995). He has been a Hayes-Fulbright Fellow (1988), studying at American University in Cairo, Egypt and Hebrew University in Jerusalem.

Contact Information:
Dr. Ralph Soney, President
Roanoke-Chowan Community College
109 Community College Rd.
Ahoskie, NC 27910
Tel: 252. 862.1308   soneyrg@yahoo.com

CALL FOR MANUSCRIPTS:
"Special Issue" & Edited Volume
Obama's Presidency: The First Four Years

The Journal of Black Masculinity is a peer-reviewed international publication providing multiple discoursed and multiple-discipline-based analyses of issues and/or perspectives with regard to black masculinities. This issue will review submissions from multiple disciplines regarding the first four years of Barack Obama's Presidency. Manuscripts will also be considered for an edited volume on the same subject. The Deadline for submissions for both JBM and the edited volume is December 31, 2011; however, we do encourage early submissions.

Manuscript submissions should be sent to Dr. C. P. Gause via the contact information below. Authors should prepare their manuscripts according to the style guide located on the website: www.blackmasculinity.com

Possible Topics:

Public Policy	Education	Healthcare
Obama-care	War Doctrine	Global Impact
Domestic Policy	Diplomacy	Faith
Obama's Swagger	Family	Historical
Reflections/Significance		
Financial Issues	Homeland Security	GLBTIQQA Issues
Patriot Act	Power	DADT-Don't Ask Don't Tell
Gender	Race	Class

The Journal of Black Masculinity ©GES Publishing Group/GES LLC
2309 W. Cone Blvd. Suite 142
Greensboro, NC 27408
www.blackmasculinity.com
www.drcpgause.com
drcpgause@gmail.com

336.509.6171

Table of Contents

This book - beyond providing educators, parents, and students with a critique of present day educational experiences for those who are the «other» in America, particularly the black male - conceptually integrates queer legal theory, the tenets of critical spirituality, and notions of collaborative activism to construct a blueprint for realizing academic achievement and academic success for all students.

Table of Contents